THE COMPLETE ILLUSTRATED ENCYCLOPEDIA OF EROTIC FAILURE

Dr Peter Kinnell

THE COMPLETE ILLUSTRATED ENCYCLOPEDIA OF EROTIC FAILURE

'I do detest conventional intercourse!'
E.M. Forster, *A Room with a View*

Futura

A Futura Book

Copyright © by Peter Kinnell 1989

First published in Great Britain in 1989
by Futura Publications, a Division of
Macdonald & Co (Publishers) Ltd
London & Sydney

ISBN 0 7088 4324 7

Printed in Great Britain by
Butler & Tanner Ltd, Frome and London

Futura Publications
A Division of
Macdonald & Co (Publishers) Ltd
66-73 Shoe Lane
London EC4P 4AB
A member of Maxwell Pergamon Publishing Corporation plc

INTRODUCTION

It's a common misconception that the life of a sexologist is an easy one, that to spend day after day relentlessly probing the soft and often unsavoury underbelly of contemporary sexuality is actually fun.

How wrong that is. This line of research can be very, very wearing, as I discovered when writing my first two books on the subject of erotic failure[1]. In fact, it was only the professional code of the Guild of Sexologists (Motto: 'All come, welcome!') that persuaded me to make myself available to those with particularly amusing failures to report. Because it's a bizarre fact that, wherever I look, there's another kink to investigate, another hilarious bedroom bungle to note down, another double-mirror to peer through.

That's the way it is with sexology — it's so damned open-ended.

At the time the call came in from my publishers, I was travelling the world on behalf of the Erotic Failures Institute and was resting up in Tahiti, where an outbreak of premature ejaculation among a beach-dwelling tribe had been reported.

The market, said my publishers, was crying out for a candid encyclopedia — the ultimate reference book of bonks that backfired.

I hesitated. Frankly, the last thing I needed was a request to return to Great Britain, the natural home of erotic failure. Did I really want to reveal to the world the pathetic sex life of the British people[2], the boastfulness of the French[3], the strangeness of the Scots[4], the over-enthusiasm of the Americans[5], the sheer horny-handed incompetence of the Australians[6]? Would I have to read the *News of the World*? Was there really anything more to say about Tony Blackburn[7]?

In the end, it was the pleas of my two Tahitian research assistants, Tiri Trivevoa and Alexis Ferulua, that decided me. These eager, willing young girls were, it transpired, desperate to join me in my probe and I simply could not find it in my heart to turn them down.

1   *The Book of Erotic Failures* and *More Erotic Failures* (Futura Publications).
2   See *WAR HERO, Prissiest, MISSIONARY, Most Easily Traumatized* etc., etc.
3   See *STATISTICAL APPENDIX.*
4   See *SEX IN SCOTLAND — A Special Supplement.*
5   See *LAW OF GRAVITY, Strangest Case of.*
6   *AUSTRALIAN WAY OF SEX, Five Most Revealing Insights into the* and *BREASTS, Most Aggressive.*
7   Yes. See *CONFESSION, Silliest Public.*

For a while, working on the encyclopedia back in England was a joy. I would spend all day expounding to Tiri and Alexis the facts of life in the West. I explained the concept of the Bimbo[8], why it was necessary to include Des O'Connor[9] in our survey, the significance of Captain Dick Head of the Paratroop Regiment[10], the danger of being hit by flying condoms while in Liverpool[11]. It was touching to see their fresh young faces cloud over as yet another aspect of western sexuality was revealed to them. Sometimes, when embarrassed by their lack of knowledge, one or both of them would offer *daihuu* (a charming tradition among Tahitian girls which involves, at moments of social difficulty, prostrating themselves on the floor, bottom in the air — sex being the solution to all problems in Tahiti). Then, as evening closed in, the girls would quite literally work me to the bone as we all relaxed with a brisk revision session.

Naturally, there were one or two problems as the book progressed. After some discussion, we had agreed that Tiri would cover books, Alexis newspapers, while I handled what in many ways is the most sensitive area of research, the first-hand, one-on-one probe (I believe I'm almost unique among sexologists in that I like to become as personally involved as possible in my cases[12] — I call this technique 'hands-on sexology').

The first hitch occurred when, tragically, Tiri caused three elderly members of the London Library to suffer from coronaries while she was looking for an obscure book of Greek Erotic Poetry on the top shelves of the T.S. Eliot Reading Room. In retrospect, it was perhaps unwise of her to insist on working in her traditional grass skirt.

Then Alexis suffered a serious humiliation in the offices of *Sunday Sport*. Because the *Sport* was not yet recognised by the Colindale Newspaper Library as a serious contribution to journalism, I had sent her to the paper's headquarters in a seedy back street of south London. There she was first refused admittance, then allowed to look through a few numbers in reception (ogled all the while by fat reporters with red braces and under-arm stains), before being ejected by the editor's secretary. Alexis, who by now was wise to British custom and tradition, tearfully remarked that to be unacceptable even to the *Sunday Sport* was the greatest humiliation that

8 See *NASAL SEX, Most Publicized Case of.*

9 See *WEDDING DAYS, Five Worst.*

10 See *PARATROOPER, Most Aptly Named.*

11 See *CONDOM CORNER.*

12 But not entirely unique. A clear example of hands-on sexology can be found under *HOLIDAY RESORT, Best Behaved,* where researchers actually fell on top of courting couples in order to ascertain precisely what they were up to. See also *WORK, Sexologist Most Frequently Interrupted While at.*

anyone could suffer. Frankly, she was never quite the same after this incident.

I was working on an essential aspect of the encyclopedia, *THE BOTTOM WORSHIPPERS' HALL OF FAME*, when we experienced the most serious crisis of the project. Tiri had been sent to the British Library Reading Room to study, reluctantly, the later writings and private life of Kenneth Tynan[13]. Her reluctance had nothing to do with Tynan, a subject she always found amusing, but was the result of embarrassment at being sat at the 'special books' table (or 'perverts' corner', as we sexologists call it). Above all, Tiri found that the official British Library rules for readers of 'special books' — one book from the sex cupboard at a time, no biros, and hands on the table at all times — to be particularly embarrassing.

On this occasion the library assistant, a good-looking young man, had fetched Tiri's book, with much noisy shaking of the cupboard keys, and had given it to her with ill-disguised disapproval. It was when she reached her place at the 'special books' table that he called out, 'Will you still be needing *A Short History of Sex-Worship* then?' Heads turned. Tiri blushed to the roots of her grass skirt. As the other readers stared at her, cultural instinct took over — she turned her back, fell to her knees and, in front of the entire library, she offered the assistant *daihuu*.

Now that Alexis had been banned from *Sunday Sport* and Tiri's case was due to come up before Marylebone Magistrate's Court, much of the joy and bounce that I had found so attractive in my assistants disappeared. They took to making unpleasant, sarcastic remarks about the British way of sex. With much chortling, they pinned on my notice-board a quotation from Fiona Pitt-Kethley's bonkologue *Journeys to the Underworld* — 'The Englishman is not an easy lay. It's not that he's any worse sexually, once you get him down to it. It's just that he takes a devil of a long time to get there. It's arguable whether he's worth waiting for.' Even our revision evenings had lost much of their spontaneity.

It was therefore no surprise when I encountered serious resistance to a suggested hands-on experiment relating to an absurd boast by Victor 'Nine-Times-a-Night' Hugo[14]. It was merely a question of simple, suck-it-and-see verification, yet for some reason Tiri and Alexis objected. Hurling

13 See *BOTTOM-WORSHIPPERS' HALL OF FAME, Top Five in the, GOING SOLO: THE GOOD AND THE BAD NEWS SUPPLEMENT, HIGH-BROW PORNOGRAPHY, Least successful Work of, MARITAL AID Oddest* and *SPANKER, Most Serious-Minded.*
14 See *STATISTICAL APPENDIX: Pathetic Boasters who Honestly Think that Quantity is More Important than Quality.*

books, notes and sexological specimens at me, they screamed that they would have nothing more to do with me or my erotic failures.

'Are you trying to tell me that you resign?' I asked calmly.

Tiri's reply was in the form of an old Tahitian saying. Roughly translated, it means, 'May your private parts turn into turnips and be rendered entirely non-functional by a Magimix Blender.' With that, my research team stormed out of the Erotic Failures Institute, never to be seen again.

Wherever they are, I thank them for their work on my behalf and forgive them for letting me down at so crucial a moment in my most important project.

Fortunately, I am still in possession of their passports, so it seems likely that they are still somewhere in Britain. If a male reader happens to come across a couple of attractive Tahitians, may I ask him to insult them roundly. If they blushingly offer him *daihuu*, they're almost certainly my girls, and should be returned to Erotic Failures Institute forthwith.

Dr Peter Kinnell
The Erotic Failures Institute

London, 1989.

ACKNOWLEDGEMENTS

Teamwork is the essence of sexology. This book could not have been completed without the help of Tiri Trivevoa and Alexis Ferulua at the Erotic Failures Institute, Marion Donaldson and Dyan Sheldon of Futura Publications' scholarly books division, and Mark Lucas of Peters, Fraser and Dunlop.

I would like to thank the following members of the Institute's hands–on design team who worked together tirelessly, sometimes into the early hours of the morning: Janette Dimond who designed, art directed and generally established the moral tone of the project; Donna Thynne for her unfailing stamina and strong stomach while researching visual aspects of the subject; Jonathan Butcher and Anne Burchell who worked on layouts all night and still had a bit of time for the book; to Stewart Larking, whose subtle drawings elevated a work which might otherwise have been seen as simply smutty; and to our lovely models 'Alan' and 'Janette' who understood the concept of erotic failure so well.

Thanks also to the staff at the British Library, the Colindale Newspaper Library, the London Library and the Kensington Library.

None of this would have been possible without the efforts, pathetic as they frequently were, of erotic failures everywhere. Well done, above all, to them.

Keep it up.

Dr Peter Kinnell

ACT OF GOD, *Oddest*

There was good news for Christian believers in Tim and Beverly La Haye's book *The Act of Marriage*. 'Years of counselling predominantly Christian couples,' wrote Tim, 'have convinced me that Christian men and women experience a higher degree of orgasmic enjoyment than non-Christians.'

In a recent survey of 151 couples within the Church, an impressive 96% of all the wives had experienced a definite orgasm at least once.

The findings of this survey were borne out by many letters happy Christian couples had sent to the authors. 'I never dreamed when I accepted Christ that he would invade our sex life,' wrote one man, 'but we had never been able to make my wife's bells ring until after we were converted. Now she has a climax most of the time.'

Sad to say, non-believers were found more often than not to be erotic failures. 'It is safe to say,' the authors conclude, 'that, except for Christians, the majority of women do not regularly enjoy orgasm in the act of marriage. In fact many don't even know what it is.'

ADVERTISING CAMPAIGN, *Least Effective*

Lincolnshire farm worker George Gregory's attempts to find a wife the easy way backfired badly when his bride, whom he had picked from a field of eleven contestants after placing an advertisement in the local paper, demanded that he take her home to her mother after a mere six days of married life.

While divorce proceedings went through, Gregory announced that his original plan to marry the runner-up had hit a snag. 'My wife Greta made me burn the letters from the ten others and I can't remember the addresses,' he said.

ADVERTISING CAMPAIGN, *Least Subtle*

A spokesman for Jiffi Condoms has denied that the company's sales slogan — 'Play it safe/Play it cool/Wear a Jiff/On your tool' — encouraged an irresponsible attitude to sex. Jiffi were particularly anxious to reach teenagers, he said, and it was therefore important to speak to them in their own language.

Supporting his case, the executive unveiled Jiffi's latest point-of-sale material — a range of products which included tee-shirts, posters and mugs, all bearing the message:

> 'If she's game
> And wants your plonker
> Wear a Jiffi
> So you can bonk her.'

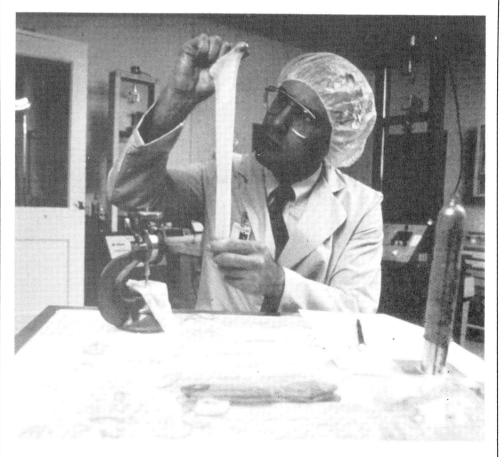

A condom-tester, wearing the traditional headgear of his profession, at work in his office. The Big Red Johnny paperweight on his desk is awarded to senior members of the condom industry

ANNOUNCEMENTS, *Ten Most Alarming Public*

ONE

Baby sister wanted. Please apply Potter's Bar.

Haringey Independent

TWO

Brassiere at Coxley Vineyard now open — Monday to Saturday.

Central Somerset Gazette

THREE

Costume jewellery business for sale. Busy site. Would exchange for six racing camels — must be pretty.

Glasgow Herald

FOUR

YOU CAN LICK OUR CHOPS BUT YOU CAN'T BEAT OUR MEAT.

Sign in a butcher's shop, Providence, Rhode Island

FIVE

Lost donkey, answers to the name of Harold. Very attractive, dearly loved by owner. Last seen in a nun's outfit.

The Bulletin, Belgium

SIX

Y-fronts wanted. No questions asked. Interesting career possibilities.

Henley Standard

SEVEN

If you are looking for a really fascinating, out-of-the-ordinary pet, may we suggest you visit the speciality section and ask to see our Miss Mortimore?

Manchester Evening News

EIGHT

FAMILY PLANNING – Please use rear entrance.

Sign outside the Barnstable Health Centre

NINE

Young farting trio (1F, 2M) seek couples, single women sharing this interest. Age, looks immaterial (over 18).

Forum

TEN

Former Navy Officer now in business, late 30s, seeks sincere lady, late or early 20s. Ex nuns or athletes given priority, any religion.

Irish Independent

ARISTOCRATIC STRIPTEASE,
The Least Likely

Travelling by train from the west country to London, the celebrated Edwardian beauty Lady Bingham suffered an indignity which was the talk of society for some months.

A stranger joined her ladyship in the carriage and, to her embarrassment, began to stare at her. After a while, he said in a low voice, 'Take off your veil.'

Being a nervous sort of person, Lady Bingham complied.

'Now take off that hat.'

She did. As the journey continued, she was obliged to take off her overcoat, her coat, her waistcoat, her blouse, her skirt, her petticoat, her camiknickers, her corset, her brassière and her boots, while the stranger stared unsmilingly at her.

She was allowed to sit naked for a while before the man pointed ominously to the luggage rack and told her to climb on to it.

'Now don't move from there,' he said.

Andover, Basingstoke, Woking — Lady Bingham lay, naked, cold and terrified on the luggage rack. She was there for an hour and a half.

As the train drew into Vauxhall, the man left the carriage without a word, stepped out on to the platform, blew Lady Bingham a kiss and was never seen again.

ART CRITIC, *Most Sex-Obsessed*

During the heady days of the mid-1960s, a group of young artists in Finchley ran a series of alternative art exhibitions which caused something of a stir in the area.

On one occasion, the chairman of the Finchley Arts Society made a surprise visit to one of their exhibitions. She walked straight past various outrageous exhibits, including a sculpture constructed out of condoms, and stood before a canvas with a single white splash on it. 'That must be removed,' she said.

When the puzzled organizers asked her why this entirely innocent picture offended, she explained that the canvas clearly portrayed a male orgasm.

The chairman's name was Mrs Margaret Thatcher.

ASSAULT, *Least Seriously Reported Case of*

Reporting on a court case in which a dentist stood accused of raping a patient, an American newspaper carried the headline, 'DENTIST FILLS WRONG CAVITY.'

AUSTRALIAN WAY OF SEX,
Five Most Revealing Insights into the
One

In November 1985, the *Advertiser* of Adelaide, Australia contained the following tribute from Mrs Beryl Holder, who had recently been widowed: 'Beryl Holder says she has no ill feeling towards her late husband, who slashed her throat and neck with a knife, stabbed her, shot her and ran her down with a car.'

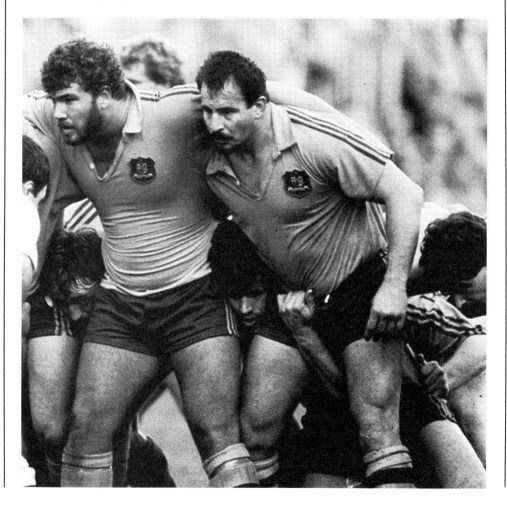

This traditional Aussie mating technique has yet to catch on elsewhere

Two

Among certain aborigine groups in Australia, it's usual for the bride to be publicly defloreated by her husband with the aid of a boomerang specially designed for the purpose, after which she is obliged to give herself to several wedding guests as a way of warding off ill health.

Three

The theory that it's the idea of sex rather than the reality of it that appeals to most men received unexpected support from Australia recently.

Speaking to the Royal Australian College of Surgeons, Dr Dan Wisniewski revealed a major breakthrough at his impotency study group in Perth: erection kits.

Of 1200 patients, no less than 300 — including an eighty-four-year-old man — had enjoyed one of three different types of implant: a bendable rod, an inflatable balloon or a complex hydraulic model which the doctor described as 'the Rolls Royce of artificial erections.'

In response to eager questioning from the floor, Dr Wisniewski explained that the cost of a new erection varied from £700 to £2700 at the top of the range. There had been no feedback from his patients' partners as to the roadworthiness of his models.

'These are the happiest patients we have ever had,' he concluded. 'They feel so good about themselves.'

Four

The following announcement recently appeared in the personal columns of *The Review* of Sydney: 'Found: Near tourist info centre, Sydney. Large white neutered male. Very friendly.'

Five

The wife of a local village rector was 'extremely emotional' when she visited the house of his churchwarden late one night, while looking for her husband, Cambridge magistrates have been told. Prosecuting counsel reported that she 'forced her way into the property and ultimately bit the man simultaneously on both arms. She was clearly emotional at the time.'

The woman was Australian, he explained.

BARMAID, *Most Easily Impressed*

Asked why, two days before her marriage to another man, she had decided to marry James Marius instead, Yorkshire barmaid Miss Dale Fishpool explained that she had reached the decision after they had finished their first kiss. 'Apart from the kiss,' she said, 'the thing that attracted me to James was his holding the title of Britain's fastest banana eater.'

BARMAID, *Most Quickly Uncovered*

Wales' very first topless barmaid lasted less than twenty minutes in her new job, a London court was told in December 1977. She was then arrested on three charges of criminal deception.

Barmaid in topless scandal: a photographic reconstruction

BED SHOW, *Least Revealing*

Foreign tourists have been shocked to the core by Soho's versions of the famous bed show and have even complained to the British Tourist Authority. Since the recent clean-up of London's most notorious red light district, bed shows normally feature a fully dressed couple sitting on a bed discussing the weather.

'I've had more excitement waiting for a train,' commented a German businessman. 'If this is an example of your British sense of humour, you can keep it.'

BEGINNERS, *Handiest Hint for Military*

A GI handbook of 1943 opened with the following important advice:

'The type of woman who approaches you in the street in Italy and says, "Please give me a cigarette" is not looking for a smoke.'

17

BETJEMAN, *John*

>>> BOTTOM-WORSHIPPERS' HALL OF FAME, *Top Five in the*, TEDDY, *Most Over-Publicized* and UNDERGRADUATE FONDLER, *Least Satisfying*.

BIBLICAL INSTRUCTION, *Most Sweeping*

Filthy beast

For many years, there was confusion among theologists as to the precise reason why Moses banned the eating of hare. Finally, the solution was found. The hare, wrote Clement of Alexandria in *The Instructor*, was well known for its habit of 'forever mounting upon its mate's crouching form . . . . The mysterious prohibition is but counsel to restrain from sexual impulses, and intercourse in too frequent succession, relations with a pregnant woman, pederasty, adultery and lewdness.'

BIG NOSES, *Best and Worst News for Men with*

Since the time of Aristotle's *Masterpiece*, men with prodigious noses have been much sought after as lovers. 'He who hath a long and great nose is an admirer of the Fair Sex,' wrote the great philosopher, 'and well accomplished for the Wars of Venus.'

During the eighteenth century, this theory was extended to women, the size of whose mouths was believed to be particularly significant. As a popular poem at the time put it:

> 'Men's tools according to their Noses grow;
> Large as their Mouths, are women too below.'

Unfortunately men big of nose and tool were not entirely blessed by nature, as the eighteenth-century sexologist Dr Nicholas de Vanette explained in his book *The Mysteries of Conjugal Love Reveal'd*:

'Admitting it true what the Physionomists say, viz. The Men with Big Noses also have stout members, as also that they are more robust and courageous than others, we have no reason to doubt at *Heliogabalus's* (whom Nature had favour'd with swinging Parts, as *Lampidus* reports) making choice of big nosed soldiers, that he might be able to undertake great Expeditions with small Numbers, and oppose his Enemy with great vigour. But at the same time he did not take notice, that well hung Men are the greatest Blockheads, and the most stupid of Mankind.'

18 >>> NASAL SEX, *Most Publicized Case of*.

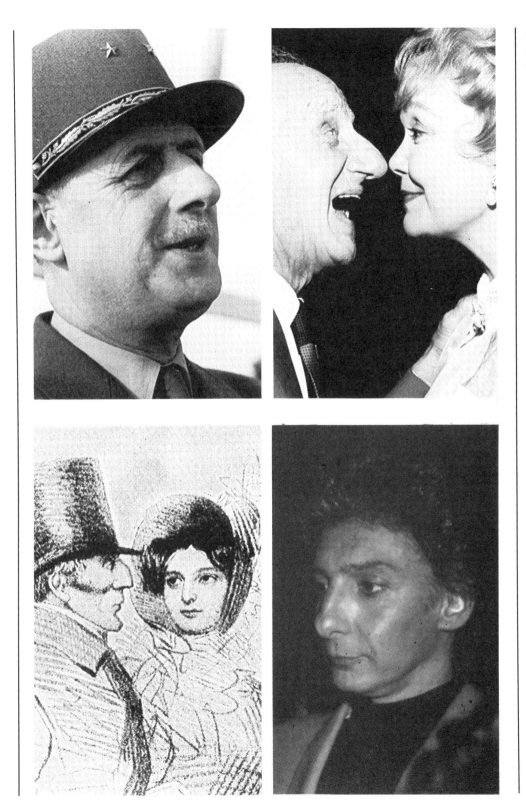

# BLACKBURN, *Tony*
>>> CONFESSION, *Silliest Public.*

BOOKSELLER, *Least Popular*

Those who attend book fairs are notorious for their lax morals and their obsession with non-literary matters, as Mr Harma N'Idan, a bookseller from Karachi, can testify.

Interviewed following extraordinary scenes at a local book fair, Harma N'Idan claimed that there would have been no problem had the Publishers Association not decided to use the Osmay Memorial Hall, a particularly decrepit building.

'Large numbers of readers were browsing when there was a power cut and the hall was plunged into total darkness,' he said. 'Muted cries and shrieks arose, and I am sure that — as happened in the same hall in 1972 — many young women lost their chastity during the cut and hundreds more were molested. I agree that no one complained, but those so injured would not dare to speak. In addition to these terrible events, over 3,000 books were stolen. Fortunately no one took a single copy of the tracts on my own stall.'

BOTTOM, *Prime Minister with Least*

It was unfortunate for Pitt the Younger that he became Prime Minister at a particularly rumbustious period of British history. Somewhat effeminate in his manner, he became known among wits at court as 'the bottomless Pitt'. The Prime Minister, it was said, 'was stiff to everyone but a lady'.

Pitt: stiff but limp

BOTTOM-WORSHIPPERS' HALL OF FAME, *Top Five in the*

'The buttocks are the most aesthetically pleasing part of the body because they are non-functional. Although they conceal an essential orifice, these pointless globes are as near as the human form can ever come to abstract art.'

Kenneth Tynan

'How brave a prospect is a broad backside!'

Henry Vaughan

'The essence of life is the smile of round female bottoms, under the shadow of cosmic boredom.'

Guy de Maupassant

'He kissed the plump mellow yellow smellow melons of her rump, on each plump melonous hemisphere, in their mellow yellow furrow, with obscure prolonged provocative melonsmellonous osculation.'

James Joyce

'Oh Hugh, may I stroke your bottom?'
John Betjeman to Hugh Gaitskell (who replied, 'Oh, if you *must*).

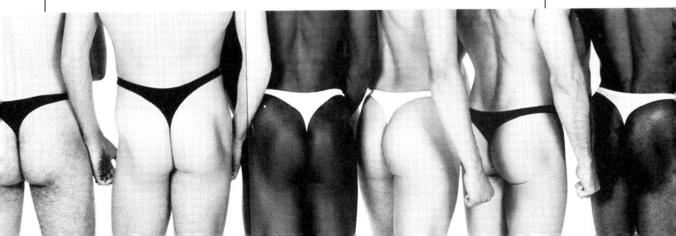

BREAKFAST PARTNER, *Least Successful*

Soraya Kashoggi, former wife of the world's richest arms dealer and darling of the gossip columns, was in confessional mood when probed by Naim Attallah for his important sociological work *Women*.

'Most men tell me that they prefer the woman to get out of bed in the middle of the night so they don't have to look at her,' she said.

Soraya: a midnight runner

BREASTS, *Most Aggressive*

'Ms Despincy's breasts are aggressive,' the *Canberra Times* reported in 1986. 'Yesterday they punched their way out of her singlet and ambushed the NSW police force. Like snipers, the breasts attacked without warning. They edged from cover, hovered dangerously, and then shot into view. Officers had to take them, and their possessor, into custody for resisting arrest and assaulting police.'

Too dangerous . . .

BREASTS, *Most Optimistic*

In a shock announcement, the mother of actor George Hamilton has revealed to the world's press that, at the age of seventy-three, she has just had her breasts enlarged by silicone implant.

'If anything happens to me,' she touchingly told her son, 'please arrange for me to be buried topless.'

BRIDE, *Prickliest*

A firm believer in reincarnation, rock star Ramma Damma claimed that his wedding at Gretna Green was the fulfilment of a dream. Although his wife was a pineapple, she had been a woman in a former life and Ramma Damma had fallen in love with her at first sight.

After the ceremony, which took place in a greenhouse, the couple slipped away for their honeymoon in a London hotel.

Too cold . . .

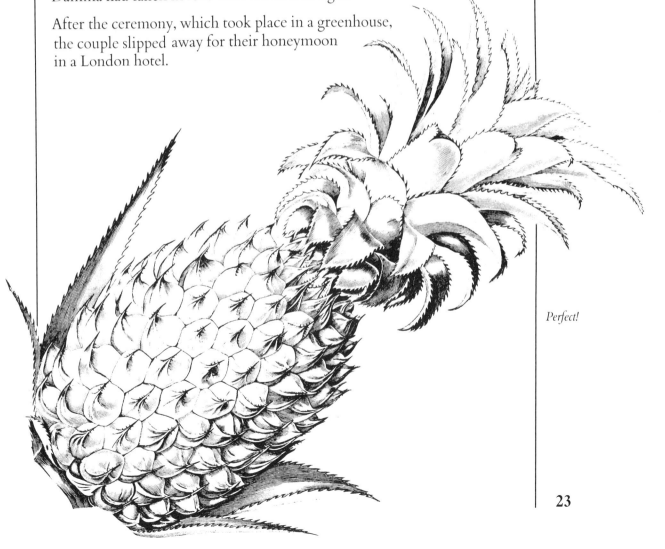

Perfect!

23

BROOKE, *Rupert*

>>> MATING RITUALS, *Ten Least Romantic.*

CANTERBURY, *Worst Behaved Archbishop of*

Bound by a vow of chastity, Thomas Cranmer, Archbishop of Canterbury during the reign of Henry VIII, kept the fact of his marriage secret for seventeen years by taking his wife about with him in a trunk full of holes.

This arrangement was uncovered when his baggage was roughly stacked by seamen at Gravesend, his wife, according to a contemporary source, being 'putt up endlonge against the wall in my Lords chamber, with the womans head downward, which putting her in ieopardy to breake her neck, she was forced at length to cry out.'

CAPOTE, *Truman*

>>> ESCORT, *Most Unreliable* and KENNEDYS, *Least Publicized Feature of.*

CENSORSHIP, *Silliest Act of*

'The steamy sex film *9½ Weeks* has been temporarily banned from Worthing's Dome Cinema until it has been privately viewed by Worthing Council's moral watchdogs,' the *Worthing Guardian* has reported. 'The film *Body Lust, The Best Bit of Crumpet in Denmark* will be shown instead.'

CHAPLIN, *Charlie*

>>> STATISTICAL APPENDIX.

CITY, *Least Romantic*

According to an in-depth survey in the *Daily Mirror*, Leeds is the English city where girls are least likely to be given a good time.

'The word "romantic" doesn't exist in the male vocabulary in Leeds,' commented secretary Claire Staniforth. 'A date means a walk round the pub and a packet of crisps if he's in a generous mood. If you're really lucky, he'll buy you a take-away.'

CLOSE ENCOUNTER, *Least Enjoyable*

Even by Hollywood's high standards, the recent revelation by Cybill Shepherd that she was used by aliens for genetic experimentation is thought to be particularly original.

The actress's unusual experience came to light when she was so worried about blank spots in her memory that she consulted a psychiatrist. Under hypnosis, she revealed how she was in her apartment when there was a blinding flash and she lost consciousness. When she awoke, she found that she was strapped down, naked, and surrounded by aliens with big ears who glowed as if there were light-bulbs inside them. One of them calmed her by saying, 'Don't be alarmed. We won't hurt you. We only need you for a genetic experiment that will help both our planets.'

Miss Shepherd was not comforted by this news, particularly since the voice of the alien speaking appeared to come from inside her.

Now that the truth has been told, the actress has come to terms with it. 'The memory of this is horrible,' she told reporters, 'but it was better knowing that I was taken by aliens than having complete blank spots in my memory.'

CONDOM CORNER

A proposal by the AIDS officer for Oxford, Mr Carl Miller, that St Valentine's Day should be re-named Condom Day was finally rejected by the council. 'We do not want to support permissiveness,' said Councillor Frederick Shellard.

I want to protest about young people throwing soggy, used condoms out of moving cars. In the last week three of these disgusting things have landed in my face, subjecting me to a higher-than-average risk of contracting AIDS.
Yours
J.L., Liverpool.
PS. My sixteen-year-old daughter says she became pregnant this way.

Sunday Sport

'Nothing but condom-power stands between the American nation and its destruction by the infernal Aids plague,' the Reverend Haron Bendo told his congregation at the Buffalo Unitarian Mission. He then distributed condoms throughout the church and led worshippers in a reading of the Ten Commandments after each of which they were obliged to recite the words, 'Condom, condom, Amen.'

ROADS COLLAPSING BUT CONDOMS ARE NO HELP
Cork Examiner

'A total failure to ensure no injurious substances would be in the product, and a humiliating experience,' was the way a Mrs Linkage summed up her feelings after discovering a condom in a tub of cottage cheese, produced by Good Foods Ltd. 'I bought the cheese in a superstore,' she said. 'One week later, while serving tea to friends, I opened the tub — and there it was.'

Pending a legal action from Mrs Linkage, Good Foods Ltd declined to comment.

During the eighteenth century, there were two main types of condom: that made from sheep's gut and the more modern linen ones, favoured by such serious seducers as James Boswell. It was thought that a job as washerwoman at Jenny's Condom Laundry was one of the less desirable jobs in London.

Former Angry Young Man John Osborne appeared to have matured into a Tetchy Old Fool when he published his autobiography **A Better Class of Person**. *Among the many people to whom he had taken an intense dislike was the charming and talented author of* **The L-Shaped Room**, *Lynn Reid Banks.*

Osborne gleefully recounts his final meeting with her. At a rather smart cocktail party, he offered her a sandwich into which he had inserted a used French letter.

'The unbelieving repulsion on her face,' writes Osborne proudly, 'was fixed for ever for me, like Kean's Macbeth.'

Osborne did not reveal how he happened to have a used French letter about his person.

'Let us always have a vast condom within us to protect the health of our soul amid the filth into which it is plunged.'

Gustav Flaubert

CONFESSION, *Oddest Form of*

The reason why the Catholic church introduced confession boxes in 1565 was not entirely because of the need for privacy — quite often, confessors were in the habit of taking members behind the altar mid-confession with the object of giving them something else to confess.

According to a letter sent by Franciscan monk Salimbene di Adamo to his fifteen-year-old niece in 1221, an attractive young girl was seldom more in danger than when being confessed. He tells the story of one woman who confessed that she had been raped by a stranger while working in the fields. The priest was so overwhelmed by her story that he dragged her behind the altar and did the same thing. When the woman tearfully confessed to another priest, he raped her as well. So did a third. The fourth time she took a knife, and obtained absolution.

And then *what happened, my dear? A father confessor at work*

Di Adamo advises his niece against taking the law into her own hands, as another penitent had. After she had been seized by a friar as she tried to make her confession, the woman suggested that there were more comfortable places to make love than behind the altar and invited him to her house the next day.

The following day, she sent him a love token in advance of his visit — a pie and some wine. It was only after the friar had generously passed the gift on to Pope Alexander IV, who was visiting the town, that the truth came out. The pie contained copious and unpleasant contributions from the woman's chamber pot.

The priest was defrocked when the Pope found out how this revolting dish came to be in the friar's possession.

CONFESSION, *Silliest Public*

'Millions buy certain newspapers so they can read about sex and boobs,' said grinning radio Romeo Tony Blackburn. 'I give it to them over the air.'

Blackburn claimed that the secret of his success on Radio London was the free and frank way sex was discussed on his programme. 'Only yesterday a cab driver told me he had driven into the back of a car when I asked a woman to twang her suspenders.'

'I love stockings and suspenders,' he continued, warming to his theme. 'I even wear them myself to prove I'm not sexist. It's all a turn-on.'

A few months later, Radio London was disbanded.

Tony: non-sexist in suspenders

CONTRACEPTION, *Least Reliable Form of*

In the first part of the eighteenth century, it was believed that knots made by sorcerers in a cord and hung around the bed could prevent conception. For this reason, wedding guests would traditionally loosen the cords on the bride's and bridegroom's clothes before they went to the nuptial bed.

Naturally there was quite a demand for knotted cords — in 1705, two people were sentenced to death for stealing them.

COSMIC EXPERIENCE, *Least Attractive*

According to the American poet and hippy guru Allen Ginsberg, his first truly cosmic experience occurred during the early 1960s. The voice of William Blake came to him as he lay masturbating and recited 'Oh Sunflower.'

COURTESANS, *Fastest Swelling*

'No women came amiss to him if they were very willing and very fat,' Lord Chesterfield wrote of the eighteenth-century monarch George I. 'The standard of His Majesty's taste made all those ladies who aspired to his favour and who were near the statuable size strain and swell themselves like frogs in the fable to rival the bulk and dignity of the ox. Some succeeded and others burst.'

COURTESAN, *Least Literary*

Born in Devon, the late-nineteenth-century courtesan Cora Pearl quickly discovered that the place for an ambitious girl to take full advantage of her beauty and shrewdness was Paris. Within months of her arrival there, she had established herself as one of the most accomplished and sought after *grandes horizontales* in Europe.

Passionately jealous of her reputation, she once fought a duel of whips with a rival, Marthe de Vere, over the affections of a Serbian prince. There was no clear-cut winner but both contestants were so badly marked that they were each obliged to wear a veil for weeks afterwards.

Pearl's greatest weakness was an insatiable greed for money. Sometimes, her avarice worked in her favour. On one occasion she bet a group of men that she was able to serve them a meat that none of them could eat. Having relieved them of their money, she retired to the kitchen. Moments later, two waiters entered with a vast dish under a great silver cover. It was Cora — stark naked.

But when an admirer, Alexandre Duval, had the temerity to present her with a book as a present, she was so insulted that she hurled it into the fire. It was only later that she discovered that the book's pages were interleaved with 1000 franc notes.

Pearl: a swinger

CRITIC, *Most Confused*

'Women are the most dangerous forces of conservatism,' wrote the literary critic Edmund Wilson in his diary. Despite reaching this momentous conclusion, Wilson spent most of his life pursuing momentous forces of conservatism with varying degrees of success.

When young, he fell in love with the poet Edna St Vincent Millais, who happened to be living with another student at the time. Wilson persuaded the couple that he should move in and that Edna should be shared. The agreement between them was admirably straightforward: her lover would enjoy the upper half of her body while Wilson very decently settled for the lower half. This arrangement did not last long.

Later in life, he still found the female sex difficult to deal with. One of the many women with whom he had an adulterous affair confessed to him that for many years she had believed that men were in a permanent state of erection because 'whenever they got close enough to her, they always were.'

CURTIZ, *Michael*
>>> FILM DIRECTOR, *Second Least Chivalrous.*

DAVID ATTENBOROUGH,
Natural Phenomenon Least Likely to be filmed by

Among the fishermen of east Africa, the most coveted catch is the dugong, a herbivorous aquatic mammal around eight foot long which not only tastes good but has sex organs similar to a woman's. According to a rather convenient superstition, a fisherman who catches a dugong is obliged to copulate with it to avoid being haunted by its spirit for the rest of his days (>>> EXCUSES, *Ten Worst*). Certain sting-rays have the same physical attributes as the dugong, but a significant disadvantage for the amorous fishermen. They sting.

The eminent sexologist J. Cleugh tells the story of a particularly attractive sting-ray being caught by an Annamese schooner off the coast of Indochina. The ship's captain, despite the presence of his wife on board, was so stimulated by the sting-ray's death throes that he threw himself on to it in a paroxysm of lust.

He was badly stung on his fisherman's friend and later died.

DEFENCE, *Most Unanswerable*

'Loisi is alleged to have severed Fisos' penis with one stroke of the knife while he was asleep in the bedroom. Her defence lawyer said it was a 'one-off' act and would never happen again.'

Auckland Star

DEFLORATION, *Clumsiest Attempt at*

During the late Middle Ages, monks and nuns appeared to take their vow of chastity rather less seriously than their counterparts today. Frequently they established relationships with one another that were less than religious.

One monk in the fifteenth century became so infatuated with a young nun that he managed to smuggle himself into her bedroom. Since the girl was a virgin, he brought with him a device to make the experience less painful for her — a board of wood with a hole cut in the middle, which he would hold between them.

The monk's plan had a flaw. At the crucial moment, he found that he was stuck fast in the wooden board. In a desperate attempt to free what a historian of the time described as her lover's 'brother Priapus', the nun went to fetch a bucket of water, thereby accidentally alerting her sisters in Christ.

Hearing voices approaching, the monk leapt through the window, still attached to the wood, and hobbled painfully back to his monastery. There his 'brother Priapus' was found to be in such a sorry state that a doctor had to be sent for.

A rare fifteenth century photography of the Brother Priapus incident. The wooden board is out of shot.

DEMONSTRATION, *Most Original*

During the campaign to convince Catholic organizers that the Pope should tour San Francisco, police were warned that a papal visit risked an unseemly demonstration. A group of homosexual nuns were planning a mass vomit-in as a protest against his refusal to recognize their order, the Holy and Universal Sisterhood of Perpetual Indulgence.

A West Coast sister mellowing out

# DICK HEAD
>>> PARATROOPER, *Most Aptly Named.*

DIPLOMATIC QUESTION, *Least*

Despite being married to a well-born Italian aristocrat, the American-born Marchesa Lulie Torrigiani was notorious in Florence during the thirties for her outrageously frank conversation.

On being introduced to a retired diplomat who had once been arrested for indecent behaviour, she asked him to turn round.

'I want to see if you wear a zipper behind,' she explained.

DOCTOR,
Country Where It is Least Advisable to Visit the

Until the relatively recent past, doctors in the country then known as Persia were known to practise traditional cures that were likely to startle the foreigner. They included:

1 For an obstruction in the anus, the doctor would insert himself;

2 For problems of male impotence, the doctor would take the organ in question in his mouth;

3 For cases of serious constipation, the doctor would allow his own private medical instrument to be sucked by the patient.

>>> **EXCUSES**, *Fifteen Weakest.*

DOMESTIC TIFF,
Least Constructive Solution to a

The final completion of Don Niblett's self-built home was not quite the happy event he had anticipated. Having spent a year and £50,000 building his own family home, DIY expert Don was devastated to hear that his wife had left him because he was not spending enough time with his family.

Having borrowed a friend's bulldozer, he drove two miles, careered through his new garden wall and flattened the house. He then destroyed the caravan in which the family had been living and his own Ford Cortina.

As police arrested him, Don was heard to shout, 'That'll show her.'

# DOUGLAS, *Kirk*
>>> **HOLLYWOOD STAR**, *Most Insecure* and **QUOTATIONS**, *Ten Least Romantic.*

ENTERTAINER, *Busiest Family*

'Dale Martin, an entertainer, has been ordered by a provincial court judge to avoid making anyone pregnant for the next three years,' reports the *Toronto Globe*. 'The order not to impregnate any girls came from Judge Leslie Bewley, who gave Martin a suspended sentence and the three-year probation for possession of an offensive weapon.'

ENTRAPMENT, *Most Unfortunate Case of*

Nottinghamshire police's tactic of using attractive and provocatively dressed policewomen as bait for kerb-crawlers recently claimed a surprising and embarrassing victim — Detective Chief Inspector Robert Warner, head of the vice and drug squad in neighbouring Lincolnshire, was arrested by a woman police constable while doing off-duty research in Nottingham's red light district.

Detective Chief Inspector Warner was bound over by magistrates and later retired from the force on grounds of ill health.

EROTIC IMAGE, *Homeliest*

Few parts of the body have been the subject of such poetic metaphors as have the clitoris. The Chinese call it 'the cock's tongue'. The Victorians called it 'the expressive button'. The Americans are fond of the terms 'buzzer' or 'bell' (as in 'You can ring my bell any time you want to'). The Irish, drawing on the Latin word 'naviculans' refer to 'the little man in the boat'.

None of these terms appealed to Dr Marian Greaves, author of the 1931 *The Mastery of Sex through Psychology and Religion*. In a game attempt to make her readers feel at home with this tricky part of the female anatomy, she wrote that it was 'much like the stump-end of a whist-card pencil.'

EROTICA, *Five Least Imaginative Noms de Plume Used by Writers of*

1 Paddy Strongcock.

2 Roland de Forrest.

3 Fuckwell.

4 L. Erectus Mentulus.

5 Clara Alcock.

EROTICA,
Five Least Promising Titles for Works of

1 Paulette de Saint-Luc, *An Up to Date Household in Paris* (1900).

2 Adam Peters, *Business as Usual* (1958).

3 Charles Sackville, *Mr Howard Goes Yachting* (1908).

4 Agnes Brickley, *Three Painful Years* (1938).

5 James Pikes, *Madwomen* (1960).

EROTICA, *Five Most Revolting Titles for Works of*

1 G.A. Bishop, *White Stains* (1898).

2 J.G. Ballard, *Why I want to Fuck Ronald Reagan* (1968).

3 Anonymous, *Cythera's Hymnal (or Flakes from the Foreskin)* (1870).

4 G. Sala, *The Frig, The Fuck and The Fairy* (1905).

5 *The Platonic Blow — Zapped and Ejaculated by two Legendary Editors and Poets at a Secret Location in the Lower East Side, New York City, USA, and Printed by the Fuck You Press for the World Gobble Grope Fellowship* (1969).

ESCORT, *Least Reliable*

When James Thurber asked the copy boy at the *New Yorker* to accompany him on adulterous assignations — Thurber had very bad eyesight by this stage in his life — he could hardly have known what a bad choice he had made. The copy boy was Truman Capote, who was to become one of the greatest gossips in the history of American letters.

Capote's role was simple enough. He had to take Thurber to the flat of one of the magazine's secretaries, wait in the living-room while they consummated their love, and then help the great man get dressed. He was eventually fired after Mrs Thurber had discovered her husband's socks were on inside out on returning from work. Thurber was convinced that Capote had done it on purpose.

'He was the rudest, meanest man I've ever seen,' Capote would tell his friends. 'He was terrifically hostile — maybe because he was blind — and everybody hated him but that one secretary he was going to bed with. She was the ugliest thing you've ever seen, but he didn't care because he couldn't see her.'

Not content with this tittle-tattle, the author of *In Cold Blood* described the sound of the couple's lovemaking as being 'as romantic as the sound of hogs being butchered.'

The twentieth century's most unlikely erotic team

EVANGELISTS, *Worst Behaved*

There's nothing new about evangelists using their saintly profession as a key to more earthly pleasures. During the fourteenth century, a travelling preacher called Segarello became notorious for acts of wanton lasciviousness. He used to roam the land with a band of like-minded clerics and a troop of whores and boys in attendance.

Segarello himself was adept at putting his religious training to full advantage. On one occasion he convinced a widow that God had ordered him to put his vows of chastity to the test by sleeping naked with her young daughter. When the woman expressed doubt, he became angry and quoted St Matthew at her: 'There be eunuchs which have made themselves eunuchs for the kingdom of heaven's sake.' She agreed to the test.

On another occasion, Segarello and two of his followers presided over a wedding. One of them announced in his sermon that it was the Lord's will that a few hours should elapse between the ceremony and the consummation of the marriage. The wife was sent to bed and, while the groom stayed drinking with his friends, the priests took turns to conduct an intimate pastoral interview with the bride up in her bedroom.

Segarello was eventually caught and burnt for heresy in 1306.

EXCHANGE, *Least Romantic*

Abdul Muni acquired a certain notoriety in his country when agreeing to exchange his wife for his brother's trumpet. 'Good trumpets are rare,' he commented. 'Women are like grains of sand in the desert.'

EXCUSES, *Fifteen Weakest*

She accepted that there had been some kissing and cuddling, but denied that she gave Larkin the impression that she was willing to spend the night with him. She agreed, however, that Larkin could have got this impression when she undressed in his room and got into his bed.

Western Morning News

I need several mistresses, if I had only one, she'd be dead inside eight days.

Alexandre Dumas

Writing in the *Electrical Trader* magazine, Dr John Saltmarsh, historian of King's College, Cambridge, has argued for a greater number of female worshippers in short skirts to visit the college's chapel to hear its famous choir. 'In the past too much of the sound was absorbed in women's long dresses,' he wrote. 'With skirts well above the knee, choral and organ music is much more resonant and rich sounding.'

A church pastor had an unhappy experience while driving around the town's red light district in an attempt to spread the gospel. The girl he first approached was Woman Police Constable Barnfather who was on surveillance duty. She arrested him on the spot for kerb-crawling.

Asked in court whether his normal pastoral technique involved the opening words, 'Do you want to have some fun?', the man replied that he wanted to make sure that he was talking to a prostitute rather than a policewoman.

When asked to explain why they had infiltrated massage parlours and escort agencies in order to offer sex for money, women from a religious cult explained that they were merely following the teachings of the New Bible.

'It's all a question of motives,' one told a reporter. 'God said "Love one another", and I'm only doing that.'

Ancient Egyptians claimed that the only way to prevent the ghost of their enemies returning to haunt them was to commit sodomy on their dead bodies.

Pleading Not Guilty to a charge of Indecent Assault, a Hong Kong man offered an unusual defence. According to the *Hong Kong Standard*, 'he told the court that he had no control over his right thumb, which had a predilection for women's buttocks.'

Asked to comment on reports that a forthcoming biography of sculptor Eric Gill would reveal that he had sex with his sisters, daughters, and the family dog, a spokesman for literary publishers Faber and Faber explained, 'He was very religious and it was part of his philosophy of life.'

The idea that sex is for procreation not pleasure, which is central to the Catholic faith, has led to some curious excesses. In his *De Excusatione Coitus*, the Catholic writer Peter Lombard argued that, since love between a man and his wife was based on desire, it was a sin — in fact, marital love was essentially more sinful than the act of adultery.

A man who got into the bed of an eighteen-year-old girl student at the Mere, Stourbridge, told police, 'I am a James Bond fan and I am adventurous.'

Worcester County Express

A man with three convictions for indecent exposure was arrested when he bared his buttocks to a group of girls. He told Balham Court last week, 'It was a stupid compromise.'

South London Press

Eskimos believe that the best way to confuse evil spirits is to change your identity. This can most easily be achieved by regular wife-swapping.

Yes, it was a dreadful thing to do, but she had very thick ankles.

Thomas Wainewright, about his murder of his sister Helen Abercrombie.

When a policeman asked thirty-four-year-old Keith Eyre why he was wearing a red mini-skirt and ladies' tights, he replied that he couldn't find his trousers, Burton Magistrates were told yesterday.

Derby Evening Telegraph

There were few surprises in a recent survey of a thousand virgin wives, whose marriage had remained unconsummated for between one and twenty years — 20% said they were afraid of the pain, 18% believed the sex act was dirty or wicked, 12% had impotent husbands, 5% were lesbians and 9% simply disliked men. But an astonishing 14% explained that their problem was caused by ignorance of the exact location of their own sex organs.

FACE-LIFT, *Most Radical*

'My agent, Giorgio Fista, was furious when he heard about it,' said Miss Jennita Zarto, a forty-year-old Bolivian actress who went into a clinic for a face-lift and was given a sex-change instead. 'But when he came to see me, he changed his mind and renamed me Johnny Zar on the spot. At first, I felt suicidal — who, after all, would choose to be a man? Then things began to look up, and I was given the part of a fisherman in a TV series.'

Denying negligence, the surgeon Dr Jaime Lurinda told local reporters, 'There is not a word of truth in the allegation that I work while on cocaine. When I saw Miss Zarto on the operating table, I thought: "She should be a man!" and set to work. I am good. I am quick. I am cheap. Everyone in the town of Chacha respects me.'

FACTS OF LIFE,
Most Traumatic Introduction to the

After a seven-year-old boy had dialled 999 and told police that his parents were having a fight, three squad cars arrived at his house at RAF Bentwaters and a number of policemen effected entry and burst into the bedroom. The couple were found to be participating in an act of love.

'We've decided to tell our boy about the facts of life,' the parents told the police.

FACTS OF LIFE,
Second Most Traumatic Introduction to

'Yes, my boyfriend and I do that every Friday night after Youth Club,' a teenage patient told her doctor, who suspected that she may be pregnant.

'I see,' he said carefully. 'And you don't think that this carries the risk of your becoming pregnant?'

'Oh no, doctor. We had biology lessons at school and I learnt all about having babies before I would let Jimmy near me.'

Confused, the doctor pressed the girl for details of these lessons.

'Well, our biology teacher said you could definitely only become pregnant if you slept with someone — and we've never ever slept together. Jimmy did get a bit dozy once, but I kept him awake.'

FEMALE LIFESPAN, *Least Scientific Theory of*

'The Womb of a Woman is in the Number of the insatiable things mentioned in the Scriptures,' wrote the eighteenth-century writer Dr Nicholas de Venette in his free and frank work *The Mysteries of Conjugal Love Reveal'd.* 'I cannot tell whether there is anything in the World, its greediness may be compared unto; neither Hell fire nor the Earth being so devouring, as the Privy Parts of a lascivious Woman.'

Hot little devil

It appeared that the privy parts of a lascivious woman were among Dr de Venette's favourite scientific subjects for he returned to them again and again throughout the book. He had a theory as to why some women are particularly amorous: 'Her genital parts . . . are a Creature in another Creature, that often causes so many Disorders in the Bodies of Women, as to oblige them to find out means to soothe and appease it, to prevent it being harmful.'

It was women's fondness for soothing and appeasing this creature within a creature that caused a shorter life expectancy than men at that time. 'They are much more amorous than men,' wrote de Venette with some feeling, 'and as Sparrows do not live long, because they are too hot and too susceptible to Love, so Women last less time; because they have a devouring Heat, that consumes them by degrees.'

FILM DIRECTOR, *Least Chivalrous*

The old charmer at work

'Which would you say is my best side, Mr Hitchcock?' the young actress Mary Anderson asked her director before her profile was photographed for the 1944 film *Lifeboat.* Alfred Hitchcock continued marking his script.

'My dear,' he said, 'you're sitting on it.'

FILM DIRECTOR, *Second Least Chivalrous*

At one time it was the habit of Michael Curtiz, the Hungarian-born director of such films as *Casablanca* and *The Adventures of Robin Hood*, to relax during his lunch-break on the set with a glass of wine, a sandwich and a spot of oral sex supplied by one of the make-up girls.

News of this behaviour reached members of the cast and crew and one day several of them crept back to the set to see for themselves. Discovered in an unbuttoned moment, Curtiz showed considerable presence of mind — he suddenly looked down at the girl with apparent surprise and disgust.

'Oh my God,' he shouted, pushing her away, 'what are you *doing* down there? Get off! Get off!'

Then he stormed off the set without another word.

FIRST LOVE, *Least Poetic Celebration of*

The Hollywood actor Peter Lawford's first experience of sex occurred when he was eleven and his French nanny seduced him. So enjoyable was it that the nanny took to inviting a woman friend to join them on picnicking expeditions on which the three of them would fondle one another in the shade of a tree. Lawford claimed that his lifelong obsession with voyeurism dated from this time.

(>>> **EXCUSES, Fifteen Weakest**.)

A poem written many years after celebrated his first love. It contained the verses:

> 'Then my nanny
> I loved her skirt
> An early start
> For such a squirt
>
> Diaper changes
> On the hour
> With penises
> About to flower.'

FIRST NIGHT SURPRISE, *Least Welcome*

In 1976, the first night of a young couple in Tulsa, Oklahoma turned out to be memorable for all the wrong reasons. In a moment of playful confession, both bride and bridegroom revealed that this was not their first time — more surprisingly, they both turned out to have slept with the same man, the Reverend Billy James Hargis, the popular right wing evangelist and founder of the American Christian College. Commenting to *Time* magazine, Hargis later admitted that he regularly had sex with men and women but put it down to 'genes and chromosomes'. After a few months, the fuss died down and the Rev Hargis resumed his Christian ministry, preaching that God was American and that rock 'n' roll was a communist conspiracy.

FISHERMEN, *Least Self-Controlled*

>>> **DAVID ATTENBOROUGH**, *Natural Phenomenon Least Likely to be Filmed by*.

FLASHER, *Least Helpful Advice to a*

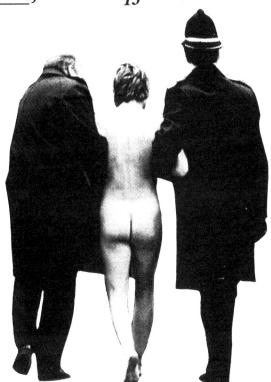

'You have been guided by the medical treatment and it's up to you to continue with it,' Mrs Mary Kessler of Bletchley Magistrates told a man convicted of exposing himself to three schoolgirls. Giving him a two years' conditional discharge, Mrs Kessler concluded, 'The matter is really in your hands.'

FRANKENSTEIN, *Most Sexual*

>>> **LOBBYIST**, *Hardest Working.*

FREUDIAN, *Least Successful*

Shortly after she met Arthur Miller, Marilyn Monroe became an avid reader of learned texts in an attempt to improve herself and her conversation. She made a particularly game attempt to come to terms with this Freud guy people were talking about.

During the filming of *River of No Return*, her co-star Robert Mitchum found her deep in a dictionary of Freudian terms. 'I feel one should know how to discuss oneself,' the actress explained.

Mitchum asked where she had reached.

'Anal eroticism,' she said.

'Charming,' said Mitchum.

Marilyn read on. 'What's eroticism?' she asked suddenly.

Mitchum explained. Another five minutes passed.

'What's anal?'

This crash course in Freudianism appears to have influenced the way Marilyn worked. Two years later, she was filming *Bus Stop* when her co-star Don Murray fluffed his lines. Instead of saying to her 'Wake up, Cherie. It's nine o'clock — the sun's out. No wonder you're so pale and white,' his last line came out as 'No wonder you're so pale and scaly.'

As the cameras reloaded, Marilyn took Murray aside and said, 'You realize what you just did? You made a Freudian slip. You see, you must be in the proper mood for this scene because it's a sexual scene, and you made a Freudian slip about a phallic symbol.'

Murray looked bemused.

'That's why you said "scaly",' said Monroe, warming to her theme. 'A snake is a phallic symbol. Don't you know what a phallic symbol is, Don?'

'Know what it is?' The actor shrugged uneasily. 'I've got one, haven't I?'

What do women want? Marilyn discusses the ultimate Freudian conundrum with Don Murray

GERTIE, *Dirtiest*

The perils of military life in Tunisia during the war are well illustrated by a popular GI ditty of the time:

> 'Dirty Gertie from Bizerte
> Had a mousetrap 'neath her shirtie
> Strapped it on her kneecap purty
> Baited it with "Fleur de Flirte"
> Made her boyfriends most alerty
> She was voted in Bizerte
> Miss Latrine for nineteen thirty.'

GIGOLO, *Least Convincing*

'I was standing at a bus stop when a woman told me I was one of the most attractive men she had ever seen, stuffed £300 in my pocket, and advised me to start a one-man escort agency,' explained Mr Daniel Hoffman, who was appearing in a south London magistrates court, charged with loitering in a public place. 'Since then I have been wined and dined by thousands of ladies, I have a flat in Lambeth and an answering machine.'

Asked whether this was his only source of employment, Hoffman said that he had continued to work as a typewriter repair man. 'It keeps me in touch with the real world and gives me something to talk about,' he said.

GOD, *Most Surprising Insight into the Power of*

In his mould-breaking work of theology *Bottom Line Catholicism for Contemporary Catholics*, bestselling author Father Andrew Greeley supplies a surprisingly up-to-the-minute insight into the attractions of the Lord.

Comparing the attractiveness of God to that of Jessica Lange in the film *All That Jazz*, he writes that 'the difference between God and Jessica Lange is not that God is less sensuous (less attractive to the human senses) but more. Ms Lange's appeal, impressive as it is, is but a hint of the appeal of the Ultimate Grace.'

GO-GO DANCER, *Saddest*

The magazine *Social Services* has recently reported a particularly tragic case:

'The social worker John Main mentioned Judy, an eighteen-year-old, pretty disturbed go-go dancer, who could not understand why she couldn't find work. Her breasts sagged. She'd lost her job. "She needs long term support," stressed Mr Main.'

GOING SOLO: *The Good and the Bad News Supplement*

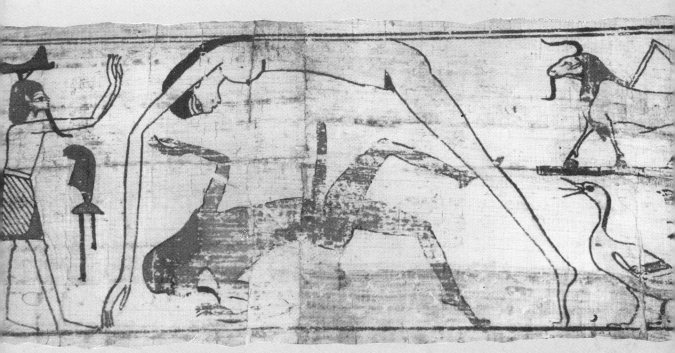

Atum Ra creates the world

THE GOOD NEWS

1

EVERYONE DOES IT

According to certain religions, the world began not so much with a Big Bang as a Big Toss. In ancient Egypt, it was believed that the god Atum Ra created the universe in a moment of spectacular, cosmic self-abuse when he 'frigged with his fist and took the pleasure of emission.' As a result, 'frigging' played an important part in Egyptian religious ritual for many centuries. Less pleasantly, they believed that the Nile was the result of the masturbatory ejaculation of the god Usiris.

2

IT'S ALL RIGHT SO LONG AS YOU KEEP YOUR THOUGHTS CLEAN

'I had no hesitation in advising the men in my unit that masturbation was perhaps the easiest and safest way of obtaining relief,' said a British medical officer, recalling active service in World War II, adding generously, 'There was no reason why they should not embellish this experience with some fantasy of their loved ones at home.'

THE BAD NEWS

1

THE DEVIL MAKES WORK FOR IDLE HANDS

According to Professor G. Hall, author of *Adolescence*, this nasty habit originates at the lowest level — from hell itself: 'Self-abuse (is) the scourge of the human race,' he wrote, 'a vice ... a perversion ... an evil ... this insidious disease ... seems to spring from the Prince of Darkness.'

2

ABSOLUTELY NO ONE IS SAFE FROM TEMPTATION

Hall had observed that even the animals indulge. Among the worst offenders are monkeys, dogs, blood stallions, elephants and, rather more surprisingly, turkeys.

You can cut that out right now

3

IT'S A MORTAL SIN

According to St Thomas Aquinas' list of deadly sins, masturbation was a more serious offence than rape, adultery or incest.

4

IT DESTROYS TEMPLES

When captive of the Philistines, Samson — described in the ancient Hebrew as a 'sahug', or phallus-beater — was forced 'to make sport of himself' while thousands watched. His dying words were 'May I be avenged to the Philistines for the draining of my fountain.'

Should they be banned?

5

IT CAN SNEAK UP ON YOU AT ANY TIME

'Among the external causes are springtime, which is a particularly dangerous season,' writes Professor Hall, 'warm climates, improper clothes, rich food, indigestion, mental overwork, nervousness, habits of defective cleanliness, especially of a local kind, prolonged sitting or standing, too monotonous walking, sitting cross-legged, spanking, late rising, petting and indulgence, corsets that produce stagnation or hyperemia of blood and great straining of the memory.'

Just in case this catalogue of forbidden activities is thought not to be comprehensive enough, Van der Velde's *Ideal Marriage* advised that a treadle sewing machine has been proved (precisely how the author fails to mention) to produce sexual excitement in some women. As for men, they 'may experience an erection while on horseback, or driving in a carriage or travelling by train; more rarely perhaps while motoring or bicycling.'

GOING SOLO: *The Bad News continued*

6
IT'S NOT TERRIBLY GOOD FOR YOU

According to Professor Hall, the average slave to self-abuse is liable to suffer from 'consumptive heredity, piles, habitual constipation, irritating urinal deposit, malformation of the organs, idleness and laziness, and weakness of the will.' For the benefit of any young reader still tempted, the professor adds, 'The masturbator's heart, so often discussed, is weak like his voice.'

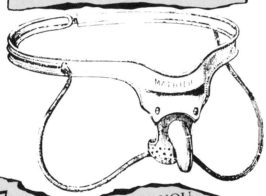

7
IN FACT, IT CAN KILL YOU

In New Haven during the seventeenth century, the crime of mutual masturbation carried the death sentence since 'it tends to the sin of sodomy if it be not one kind of it.'

8
OR AT LEAST DRIVE YOU MAD

A 1901 survey of 800 cases of insanity in the New York State Insane Asylum revealed that 107 were addicted to this practice. Surprisingly it was thought that it was these patients, rather than the majority who abstained, that were in serious need of treatment.

9
SCIENTISTS HAVE TRIED TO PUT A STOP TO IT (WITH DISASTROUS RESULTS)

During the nineteenth century, the task of preventing young males from playing with themselves became one of the great scientific challenges of the age. The Germans, then as now pioneers of high technology, led the way with a simple clasp device, invented by S.G. Vogel, to be attached to the foreskin. The general feeling was that the Vogel clip was only partially successful and J.L. Milton in his 1887 bestseller *Spermatorrhea* advocated a steel girdle, for which the parents of teenagers would keep the key or a cage lined with spikes to discourage unauthorized erections. If these devices were thought to be unsuitable for nighttime use, Milton suggested the use of a simple electrical device by which any filial erection rang a bell in the parents' bedroom.

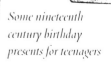

Some nineteenth century birthday presents for teenagers

10

BOY SCOUTS DO IT

The great cubmaster Baden-Powell had little patience for boys who were tempted to do things to themselves. His great work *Rovering to Success* contains some brisk words of warning: 'You are throwing away the seed that has been handed down to you as a trust instead of keeping it and ripening it for bringing a son to you later on.' His only other advice concerning matters below the belt is: 'Keep the racial organ cleaned daily.'

11

YOUR PARENTS CAN ALWAYS TELL

In 1877, Dr John Harvey Kellog of Battle Creek, Michigan used to lecture on the theme 'Do you know what your children are doing' and provided thirty-nine tell-tale signs for parents concerned that their children were indulging in vice. They should be particularly alert if their teenage girls lacked breast development, had pimples on the face (particularly on the forehead), bit their fingernails, ate clay, slate, pencils, or chalk, or had habitually cold, damp hands.

12

IT'S THOROUGHLY UNPATRIOTIC

During the First World War, it came to the notice of the authorities that a certain amount of unauthorized self-abuse was taking place in the armed forces. In 1919, the Reverend B.W. Allen explained that it was the soldier's duty to his country to leave himself alone. 'When temptation comes, as come it will to all,' the Rev. Allen wrote in his aptly named 'ejaculatory prayer', 'find strength in this: "I cannot give way, I cannot give way: I am the son of a King — of God".'

American sailors during World War II were more fortunate and were actively encouraged to keep their libido in check by regular light relief. As the popular song went:

'Masturbation is the fashion
For your unrequited passion.
If the girls can do it, why can't we?
But out here in the Pacific,
Purely as a soporific.
Nothing equals simple self-abuse.'

BP: Rovering with young friends

15

SCIENTISTS HAVE TRIED TO HELP YOU DO IT (WITH DISASTROUS RESULTS)

As the rhythm of research into this important area of human behaviour has quickened over recent years, so has the technological back-up. Dr William Hartman's and Marilyn Fithian's *Any Man Can* gives an exhaustive account of how painstaking solo work can help men achieve just as many multiple orgasms as women. The authors recommend various masturbation machines on the market, including the Acujack, a handy portable false vagina which is powered by electricity or the cigarette-lighter outlet of a car, and they particularly recommend a device patented by Funways Inc.

But they conclude with a sobering note of warning to high-tech onanists: 'NEVER set the machine too fast.'

13

IT CAN BE DAMNED HARD WORK

Now that attitudes to self-abuse have come full circle, it's easy for the modern masturbator to regard it as a matter to be tossed off in a few minutes. Nothing could be further from the truth as *The Sensuous Woman*, a seminal work of sexology, reminds us: 'Set aside several hours a week for masturbation so that your response pattern will become a stable one' is the firm instruction.

14

IT'S SEXIST

According to the 1975 *Sexual Attitude Restructuring Guide*, writers on this important subject should no longer use the term 'jacking off' when the subject happens to be feminine. On these occasions (which, for sensuous women, are frequent), the correct usage is 'jilling off'.

16

IT CAN PLAY HAVOC WITH MOTORWAY TRAFFIC

According to his widow Patricia Seaton Lawford, the actor Peter Lawford became increasingly dependent on hi-tech solo sex aids during the latter part of his life. This was because, until science lent a hand, he could only achieve orgasm after several hours of oral sex, involving at least two women. Even with the obliging Patricia, this was not always practicable.

Lawford's experience showed that there were distinct advantages and disadvantages to the handy Acujack device which he bought from a sex shop. The advantages were:

a) that it never said 'no';

b) that it kept going all night long after a mere woman would have collapsed with exhaustion, lockjaw or chronic boredom.

The disadvantages were:

a) that it made a noise like a kitchen blender and its all-night droning kept the rest of the house awake;

b) that it looked extremely silly;

c) that a normal male orgasm, achieved when the Acujack was attached to a car cigarette lighter, could cause a short circuit, followed by a massive and electric shock.

It was when a fellow Acujack-lover careered off a motorway and drove into a tree, killing himself, that Peter Lawford decided to abandon technology and return to the simple Hollywood pleasure of prolonged group sex and voyeurism.

17

THESE DAYS, EVEN LITERARY ROLE MODELS DO IT

Onanism is particularly popular among writers, it's claimed. The critic Kenneth Tynan, who told his wife that 'I write to be sexually desirable', would regularly abuse himself before a day's writing, as did Dylan Thomas. More recently, Anthony Burgess has confirmed the close connection between creative and onanistic impulses. 'Writers are the most masturbatory of creatures,' he told a startled interviewer on BBC's Radio Four. 'Ask any writer — they're like monkeys.'

18

IT CAN CAUSE YOU TO MAKE AN AWFUL MESS OF YOUR FAVOURITE MAGAZINE

In spite of modern advances, traditional methods retain their popularity — although there's always room for new variations on the old theme.

'I have tried various ways of tossing off whilst looking at the pin-up in Fiesta,' a Mr A.C. of Scotland wrote to that magazine, 'but it is very difficult to hold the page with one hand. How about having a Fiesta centre page pull-out with a hole cut through the middle with a French letter fixed behind a sponge cushion. This could be then pinned on a mattress and given a right going over.'

GOVERNMENT,
Strongest Believer in Smack of Firm

The great nineteenth-century statesman and philanderer Lord Melbourne was cited twice in divorce cases during his political career which, while it caused a certain frostiness in his relations with Queen Victoria, did not prevent him from being her greatest confidant during the years when he was Prime Minister.

Less objectionable at the time than his conventional indiscretions was his eager interest in the subject of flagellation — *le vice anglais* had reached a peak of popularity at the time and was generally thought to be an acceptable hobby among the upper classes. 'No mother really loves her children who never does it,' he wrote to one of his mistresses, Elizabeth Brandon, who shared his enthusiasm for the whip. As confirmation of his interest in the well-being of young people, he used to send her pictures of children being thrashed.

Melbourne was particularly concerned in the discipline of young female domestic servants. 'It is difficult to produce much effect upon the thick skin of a dog covered with hair,' he wrote to Miss Brandon. 'But a few twigs of birch applied to the naked skin of a young lady produce with very little effort a very considerable sensation.'

Melbourne explains his controversial 'Random Spanking of Naughty Housemaids Act' to Queen Victoria

GRAND DUCHESS, *Randiest*

A familiar sight on the French Riviera during the 1930s was the eminent white Russian exile, the Grand Duchess Anastasia, trawling the local bars and beaches for young men. Having found one who suited her purpose, she would take him back to her villa in Eze. A few days later, the Grand Duchess's latest victim would be ejected, pale and spent.

'She is like measles,' one commented gamely. 'Everybody should go through the experience. Once you've had it, you never want to have it again.'

GRANT, *Ulysses S.*

>>> PRESIDENTIAL BEHAVIOUR, *Least Appropriate.*

GREATEST BLOCKHEADS, *Well-Hung Men as*

>>> BIG NOSES, *Best and Worst News for Men with.*

GREER, *Germaine*

>>> MATING RITUALS, *Ten Least Romantic.*

HALPERN, *Sir Ralph*

>>> STATISTICAL APPENDIX.

HANGOVER SYMPTOMS, *Most Unusual*

The nineteenth-century traveller Sir Richard Burton, who had a pronounced interest in the sexual habits of foreigners, was told of a particularly unpleasant punishment favoured in Persia. If a man was discovered in a harem or 'Gynaeceum', he was made to strip and surrender to the less than tender embraces of the grooms and negro slaves.

'I once asked a Shirazi how penetration was possible if the patient resisted with all the force of the sphincter muscle: he smiled and said "Ah, we Persians know a trick to get over that; we apply a sharpened tent-pole to the cropper bone (*os coccygis*) and knock till he opens".'

Burton tells the story of the Governor of Bushire, 'a man famed for facetious blackguardism', who liked to invite young European officers serving in the Bombay Marines and 'ply them with liquor till they were insensible.' The next morning (after a night of the long tent-poles) they would awake with the most unusual form of hangover, complaining that 'the champagne had caused a curious irritation and soreness in *la parte-poste*'.

HEAD, *Dick*

>>> PARATROOPER, *Most Aptly Named.*

HEADLINES, *Five Most Worrying*

1. ## ONE-LEGGED ESCAPEE RAPIST STILL ON RUN
   Bournemouth Evening Echo

2. ## MAN WHO ATTACKED WOMAN MAY HAVE THOUGHT SHE WAS HIS WIFE
   Macclesfield Express Advertiser

3. ## VIRGIN'S NEAR MISS WITH A WHALE
   Weekend Australian

4. ## TEEN PREGNANCY: BOYS ARE HALF THE PROBLEM
   New York Post

5. ## TWO SEX FILMS TO BE VETTED BY PLYMOUTH'S FIRE BRIGADE COMMITTEE
   Plymouth Herald

HIGH-BROW PORNOGRAPHY,
Least Successful Work of

In 1971, the critic and sexual enthusiast Kenneth Tynan was paid $7500 by Grove Press to compile an anthology of masturbatory pieces by eminent writers. Unfortunately, none of the authors approached shared Tynan's interest in sex writing.

'I have no interest whatever in pornography and cannot imagine being titillated by what I write,' was Vladimir Nabokov's reply. Graham Greene wrote a curt note, saying, 'I'm afraid I don't feel like joining this children's game.' W.H. Auden was similarly dismissive. 'There are a number of things which one does not want to put into a book, and pornography is one,' he wrote. Even Norman Mailer, who was not above including explicit sex scenes in his novels, found the project distasteful. 'I'd never write to arouse my own sexual impulse,' he told Tynan. 'I don't even know if I can wish you well on your book.'

>>> **GOING SOLO: THE GOOD AND THE BAD NEWS SUPPLEMENT**.

HIPPIES, *Most Confused*

In his book, *The Marching Eros*, the Indian author Som Deva warns his readers about some of the sexual habits of the alternative society.

'One may see a girl in her mother-nakedness dancing around a hippy guy,' he writes, 'and another looking at the spectacle with passing amusement. Her boobs and the hirsute "pelvic triangle" look prominent in the soliciting gestures.'

Unfortunately, Deva adds, 'The hippies have their own sexual problems. If a girl shows favour to one while sexually interlocked with the other one clamours for justice. The number of men they take for the jaunt are legion. Some of them break in the middle and they go back to civilization to be rooted there again. They can't understand it, simply they can't.'

# HITCHCOCK, *Alfred*
>>> **FILM DIRECTOR**, *Least Chivalrous.*

HOLIDAY RESORT, *Best Behaved*

Encouraged by reports that Blackpool was a hotbed of sexual activity, the Mass Observation unit, who were studying the everyday life of Britain in minute detail, sent a squad of twenty-three observers there during the summer of 1937. Armed with pencils and pads, they posed as holidaymakers and mingled among couples on the beach, looking out for any hint of light or heavy petting, carefully noting it down and timing its duration.

The final statistics made disappointing reading. On one evening between eleven-thirty and midnight, they spotted 232 cases of petting, ranging from 'Sitting down and embracing' (120) to 'Necking in cars' (9), but the Observation Unit had been unable to discover any actual instance of full-blown sexual intercourse.

Determined that Blackpool's lovers would not get off so lightly, the observers took to the sand dunes. 'Observer units combed the sands at all hours,' one of the amateur sexologists reported. 'They pretended to be drunk and fell in heaps on located sand couples to feel what they were doing exactly, while others hung over the sea-wall and railings for hours watching couples in their hollowed out sandpits below. Lines of observers systematically beat the notorious sand dunes . . . . All the alleged sex areas were covered in this way.'

A uniformed inspector attempts to blend in with the crowd

60

Sadly, despite their efforts, the sum total of full sexual incidents to be reported after several weeks of sneaking up, watching and falling on top of couples, was four — and one of those involved an observer.

In its report, the Mass Observation unit described Blackpool as 'the most moral town in England.'

HOLIDAYMAKER,
Most Comprehensively Fleeced

A number of British tourists have become victims of a 'sicko Spaniard with a hairdressing fetish,' according to the *Sunday Sport*. Following what the paper describes as a 'series of Barber of Seville-style attacks' on the Costa Brava, police are looking for a young Spaniard who chats up fair-haired British women before drugging them. When they awake, they find that their private parts have been shaved.

While most of the victims are in their twenties, it was a forty-seven-year-old housewife, holidaying without her family, who first alerted police to the problem. 'This is the first and last time I will ever take a separate holiday from my husband,' she told reporters. 'I woke up surrounded by rude polaroid photos of myself with my private area shaved. I was never so shocked in my life. The first thing I thought was "How am I going to explain this to my Harry?"'

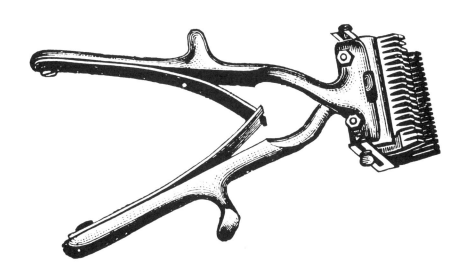

HOLLYWOOD STAR, *Most Insecure*

In his autobiography, *The Ragman's Son*, Kirk Douglas is at pains to point out that his success on screen has been nothing compared to his sexual achievements, but perhaps his most revealing moment of self-knowledge is to be found in a sad note towards the end of his book.

'An erection is a mysterious thing,' he writes. 'There's always that fear, each time one goes, that you won't be seeing it again.'

Kirk: no mysterious thing

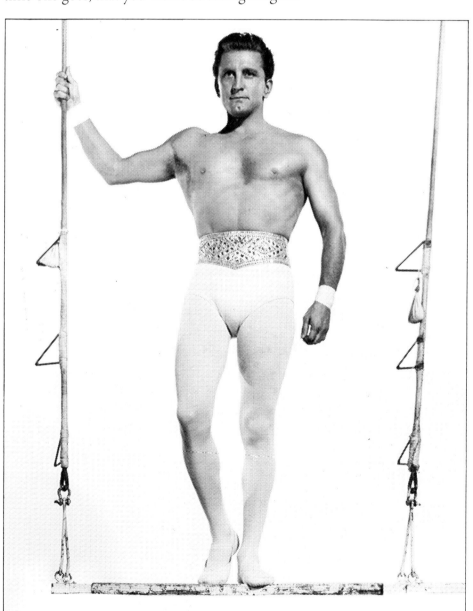

HOLY AND UNIVERSAL SISTEHOOD OF PERPETUAL INDULGENCE, *The*

>>> DEMONSTRATION, *Most Original.*

HORIZONTAL RECRUIT, *Most Reluctant*

'The underground was rather shy and inhibited,' said writer and commentator David Robins when asked by Jonathon Green about sex in the sixties. 'Later, though, when "horizontal recruitment" became the more favoured form of recruitment on the libbo Left, then it really did get going. The libertarian loony Left scene of the early 70s was very strong on rogering and leg-over: it was a leg-over-based scene.'

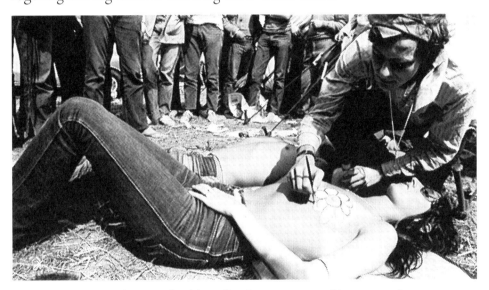

A really beautiful scene: a sixties leg-over artist at work

The painter Nicola Lane had less fond memories of horizontal recruitment. 'What it meant was that men fucked around. You'd cry a lot and you would scream some time, and the man would say, "Don't bring me down — don't lay your bummers on me . . . don't hassle me, don't crowd my space".'

'Sex was my drug,' recalled ardent recruiter Jim Haynes. 'I had a revelation in the early 60s that sexuality, when it was positive, was one of the greatest sources of human pleasure, ever.'

This again was not quite how Nicola remembered it. 'Jim Haynes tried to sleep with me. I wasn't alone, there were about six other women in the bed. I said "No". He humiliated me . . . . I'd love to meet Haynes again, now that he's a shrivelled-up old man, and humiliate him in the way that he humiliated me.'

63

HOUSE GUESTS, *Worst Behaved*

Edwardian society weekend parties were noted for the feverish bed-hopping that traditionally took place after the guests had retired for the night. But, well-organized as these adulterous events were, there were still occasional misunderstandings.

A bishop and his wife, for example, were startled to be awoken at three o'clock in the morning by a naked man flying through the air and landing on the bed between them with a loud cry of 'Cock-a-doodle-doo!' It was Lord Beresford. He was in the wrong room.

Lord Cardigan showed rather more *savoir faire* when visiting the wife of a fellow-guest who was, he believed, downstairs drinking port. He was just about to slip into the woman's bed when the door opened. It was her husband.

'Hush!' said Cardigan without a moment's hesitation. 'Don't wake her. I thought I smelt smoke, but all's well.'

'Good show,' said the grateful husband.

A typical Edwardian scene

HUSBAND, *Most Long-Suffering*

Opposing his wife's petition for divorce, Mr Gerald Digby admitted to the court that all had not been well in the Digby household for some time. After his wife Gay had begun to suspect that he was taking tea, semolina and other items from the pantry and tampering with her clothes in the wardrobe, she had fitted locks to all the doors in their fourteen-room house, which was 'like Fort Knox'. On one occasion, it had taken him over two hours to find one of the keys because she kept changing the hiding places.

Seven years ago, Mr Digby continued, his wife had put a stop to all sexual intercourse because she had an allergy and was afraid of developing a rash.

Mrs Digby's petition for divorce was dismissed by the court. 'I still want my wife and will be doing everything to get us back together,' Mr Digby told reporters.

ILK, *Least Chivalrous Scotsman of that*

>>> SEX IN SCOTLAND.

INCUBUS, *Most Determined*

In 1491, scandal broke out at a monastery in Cambrai, France when one of the nuns reported that she had been seduced by an evil spirit in the form of a handsome young man, no less than 444 times. Not satisfied by these carefully documented seductions, the incubus then demanded an introduction to the other nuns in the monastery and had chased them about the monastery gardens, forcing them to climb trees to escape from his evil intentions.

>>> PARANORMAL EXPERIENCE, *Least Rewarding*.

INSEMINATION, *Last Word on*

'The artificial insemination of animals is taken for granted to improve the breed and product,' reported the *Catholic Register* of Canada. 'Human insemination is a different ball-game.'

INTELLECTUAL ACHIEVEMENT, *Most Conclusive Proof of the Connection Between Pecker Problems and*

In his startling book *Intellectuals*, the historian and *Daily Mail* columnist Paul Johnson advanced his highly original genital-based theory of western culture.

The theory goes as follows:

1 The philosopher Jean-Jacques Rousseau had a small and deformed penis.

2 The playwright Henrik Ibsen was so embarrassed about his penis that he refused even to show it to his doctor.

3 The publisher Victor Gollancz developed a fear that his penis disappeared into his body every time he sat down and took it out several times a day to check that it was still there.

4 Rousseau, Ibsen and Gollancz were intellectuals. So were Tolstoy, Sartre, Bertrand Russell and Edmund Wilson, all of whom had sexual hang-ups.

5 Therefore, while all people suffering from problems with their genitals are not necessarily intellectuals, intellectuals will almost certainly suffer from problems with their genitals.

6 Do not trust intellectuals.

7 If you are tempted to go to bed with an intellectual, forget it. Go to bed with someone normal, a *Daily Mail* columnist for example, instead.

No, I'm not an intellectual!

INTELLIGENCE, *Least Intelligent Act of*

It was all most irregular but British Intelligence thought it was worth a try. Convinced that the French negotiations with the Italians at Aix-les-Bains during World War I were at their expense, special agents were despatched to discover what had been discussed and decided. They concluded that, since they were dealing with continentals, sex was the best weapon.

The operatives did their research. Pichon, the French foreign minister, was unfortunately thought to be above temptation but his opposite number, an elderly Italian marquess, was said to be highly sexed, if a little odd.

Acting on information received, the agents hired a plump blonde local woman whose brief was simple: to suggest to the marquess that they hold an orgy in his hotel suite. Once she had persuaded him to entertain her, all she would be required to do was to appear in a low-cut white gown and cut the head off a cockerel, which would be provided.

All went well until the girl seductively closed in on the cockerel bearing a knife. It fought back, attacking her. Hearing screams from the hotel room, British Intelligence burst in to find the girl, half-naked and in a state of collapse, the marquess in a state of dazed ecstasy and the cockerel about to breathe its last.

The agents ransacked the room, finally discovering the minutes of the meeting in the marquess's trouser pocket. It was another great triumph for British ingenuity.

INTERPRETATION OF THE BIBLE,
Most Drastic

The elders of the Skopzi sect in Russia based their creed on St Matthew XIX.12:

'For there are some eunuchs, which were so born from their mother's womb; and there are some eunuchs, which were made eunuchs of men: and there be eunuchs which have made themselves eunuchs for the kingdom of heaven's sake. He that is able to receive it, let him receive it.'

Quite clearly, according to the Skopzi, true believers were obliged by this text to castrate themselves — indeed, they believed that only if 144,000 men had been converted in this way would Jesus return to earth.

Not surprisingly this news failed to convince some sceptical individuals to take the knife to themselves and, as the magic figure of 144,000 appeared more and more unattainable, religious ceremonies among the Skopzi became increasingly violent and sado-masochistic, even involving the amputation of the breasts of virgins.

A more agreeable Russian sect was The Ticklers, at whose religious services male worshippers were obliged to tickle the nearest female until she fainted.

INTERPRETATION OF THE BIBLE,
Most Literal

>>> **Excuses**, *Fifteen Weakest.*

INTERPRETATION OF THE BIBLE,
Oddest

There is good and bad news for Christian couples in Tim and Beverly La Haye's book *The Act of Marriage.*

The bad news is that no sex act is permissible within a marriage that is not sanctioned by the Bible.

The good news is that, with careful reading, quite a lot is in fact allowed. The La Hayes quote The Song of Solomon II:6 — 'Let his left hand be under my head, and his right hand embrace me.' This, they say, is a clear reference to manual stimulation of the clitoris.

>>> **ACT OF GOD**, *Oddest.*

Christian marriage: anything goes

ITEM OF PALACE REGALIA,
Least Frequently Worn

The Tanna tribespeople of the Vanuatu Islands have many interesting beliefs and traditions, the most eccentric of which is thought to be that they regard Prince Philip as a god. Dr Martin Fisher, a scientist visiting the tribe in order to research the rapid spread of the Hepatitis B virus, discovered how seriously the tribe take their religion when he was asked to take a twelve inch penis sheath and deliver it to the prince as a token of the Tanna people's respect.

On hearing of Dr Fisher's mission, a Buckingham Palace spokesman pointed out that, since the god was not in residence, he would not be able to accept it personally. The sheath could however be delivered to the Palace — by a side-door.

JAGGER, MICK,
Taken from the Rear by Cecil Beaton

>>> **ROYAL PHOTOGRAPHER**, *Most Affectionate.*

JEALOUS REVENGE, *Least Logical Act of*

'The night after a young wife returned home without her skirt her husband made her eat a moth.'

Sheffield Star

JIFFI CONDOMS

>>> **ADVERTISING CAMPAIGN**, *Least Subtle* and **SAFE SEX**, *Five Most Misguided Contributions to.*

JILLING OFF

>>> **GOING SOLO: THE GOOD AND THE BAD NEWS SUPPLEMENT.**

JILTED BRIDEGROOM, *Most Swiftly*

An easy-going, modern-minded man, Paul Clarke decided not to make too much of a fuss when his bride Elaine disappeared twice for lengthy periods during their wedding reception.

But even Paul was surprised later as his best friend Robbie Witts drove the happy couple to their honeymoon hotel. Elaine admitted she had slept with another man the previous night and that she was having an affair — with Robbie Witts.

At that moment, Robbie stopped the car and invited Elaine to join him in a lay-by where they made love, as Paul looked on helplessly.

'We never actually consummated the marriage,' he said later. 'So maybe we can get an annulment.'

>>> **WEDDING DAYS**, *Five Worst.*

JOHNSON, *Paul*

>>> **INTELLECTUAL ACHIEVEMENT**, *Most Conclusive Proof of the Connection Between Pecker Problems and.*

JOURNALISTIC CONTRIBUTIONS TO EROTIC FAILURES, *Top Ten*

ONE

Marie, a member of Bournemouth and District Outdoor Club, has been campaigning for a nudist beach for fourteen years. Joining her in the plea is the Naturist Foundation, who'd also like a section of the beach where its members can hang out.

Bournemouth Evening Echo

TWO

It is a serious offence and we would like anyone who saw a naked man yesterday, or on any other occasion, to contact us immediately, police said.

Birmingham Daily News

THREE

Toronto: The first sex-change operation in Canada has been performed at Toronto General Hospital on an anonymous in-patient whose sex is being withheld.

Hospital Times, Toronto

FOUR

And he's not such a devil with women as the Sean Connery-style Bond. In fact he's actually the daughter of a kind of Mafia-boss — Diana Rigg looking gorgeous in a see-through wedding-dress — and confines his pre-marital affairs to almost a business-only confrontation.

Sheffield Star

FIVE

'Yesterday, there were reports of young men and women prancing around absolutely naked,' said Alderman Oxford. 'I wonder what would be thought if members of this committee turned up naked — there would certainly be a feeling of revulsion.'

Staffordshire Sentinel

SIX

ARE YOUR COOK'S DRAWERS REALLY GOOD ENOUGH?

Just go into the kitchen and make a swift check of the cook's drawers. Are they really the sort of thing you want around your food while it is being prepared? Can you remove them easily? Could you wash them or even wipe them clean without a lot of frustration?

Focus on Rickmansworth

SEVEN

Mrs Maureen Trunks of Costead Manor Road, Brentwood, who claimed that she had been raped by a Metropolitan Policeman, admitted wasting police time today.

Southend Standard

EIGHT

Last week, 21,000 high school boys got a girl pregnant.

National Enquirer

NINE

A prostitute with pink plastic curlers atop her head and carpet slippers on her feet did the meringue through the door and all the way to a can of Crisco. She picked it up, danced back to Mr Polnco, and asked for a pack of Newport cigarettes. Then she paid, stuck out her tongue, put her thumbs in her ears, and wiggled her Continued on page 47, column 4.

New York Times

TEN

A motorist driving down Evesham Road in Crabbs Cross in the early hours of Sunday morning was surprised to see a man standing by the roadside naked except for a sheet 'which he opened from time to time.' A subsequent police search revealed nothing.

Redditch Indicator

KARATE KING, *Most Caring*

'The girls want to call me Master and fall at my feet,' film star Jackie Chan, known to martial arts fans as 'the Chinese Rambo', modestly revealed in a recent interview.

So jealous are his female fans that Chan's film contracts forbid him from kissing on screen or having affairs with his co-stars.

'I daren't wed,' confessed the karate star. 'There would be mass suicides among my fans.'

An Egyptian wife recovers from a weekly visit from a 'key'

KENNEDYS, *Least Publicized Feature of*

'What I don't understand is why everybody said the Kennedys were so sexy,' said that model of indiscretion, Truman Capote. 'I know a lot about cocks — I've seen an awful lot of them — and if you put all the Kennedys together, you wouldn't have one good one.'

Capote went on to reveal that, when staying with friends on Palm Beach, he had the opportunity — which, naturally, he took — of spying on Jack Kennedy as he bathed in the nude. 'He had absolutely nuthin!' was the verdict. 'Bobby was the same way; I don't know how he had all those children. As for Teddy — forget it.'

KEY, *Least Publicized*

Newly wed husbands in ancient Egypt had a problem. They insisted on marrying virgins, and yet were squeamish about the messy business of defloration, which they found distasteful and undignified. As a result, many of them used to employ a freelance operator known as a 'key' — usually a powerfully built Abyssinian with a reputation for sexual brutality.

Keys made additional money from selling the blood-stained sheets to the husband, who would then proudly boast of his wife's purity before marriage.

Over the centuries, the practice of using keys became commonplace throughout north Africa.

Frequently, wives were not satisfied by the one performance and 'keys' achieved legendary status within the community. Historians record that the most famous key — a man who boasted that he could knock a man down with his penis, which was as thick as a man's wrist — was killed when his luxurious residence was hit by a shell during the siege of Khartoum in 1884. It is said that a number of Sudanese women committed suicide following the event and a rich local widow actually bought the dead man's famous organ for her own private use.

KICK FROM A DONKEY, *Kiss Most Similar to*

Something very strange happened to men who kissed Margarita Santos of Atlantic City in America. Their heads swam, everything went black and they lost their wallets.

Margarita, a local prostitute, was arrested when several of her clients complained about this unadvertised aspect of her service. According to local police, Margarita's trick was to carry small plastic bags of anaesthetic in her mouth which burst on contact. They were unable to explain why the drug only worked on punters, not on Margarita herself.

LAID GHOST, *Most Frequently*

Following a lead story in the *People* concerning the amorous activities of a ghost in Worksop, the newspaper was obliged to print a public apology to the ghost's brother.

The paper's allegation was certainly serious enough. It claimed the spirit in question had taken to climbing into bed with eighteen-year-old Beryl Gladwyn in the early mornings. It then fondled her, kissed her, and bit her neck. Because the ghost came to bed wearing boots, it was assumed that, before it passed over, it had been a miner.

A local clairvoyant was rash enough to go further. He claimed that the randy ghost was almost certainly the spirit of a pitman called Dexter, who used to live there. It was this libel that Mr George Dexter, brother of the alleged ghost and groper, objected to.

The clairvoyant was unrepentant. 'I fear this presence will try to make love to Beryl if something is not done,' he told reporters. 'I plan to try to lay this ghost as soon as conditions are right.'

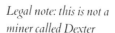

Legal note: this is not a miner called Dexter

LANGE, *Jessica*

>>> GOD, *Most Surprising Insight into the Power of.*

LAST RITES, *Oddest*

When a woman's husband dies in Kipolom, a small island between New Guinea and Australia, his widow's problems are only just begining. By tradition, she is obliged to lie in her late husband's freshly filled grave and copulate with every man in his totem group.

It is believed that this practice has a doubly beneficial effect: the husband's spirit is made to understand that he is truly dead and therefore it should not haunt the tribe, while the widow is shown that she is now at the disposal of any other man in her group.

LAW OF GRAVITY, *Strangest Case of the*

Appearing in a court in Houston, Texas on a charge of invading a baseball pitch, topless dancer Morganna Roberts claimed that the law of gravity was to blame. One moment she was leaning over a fence, the next her sixty-inch bust just toppled her over. Then she got up, ran on to the pitch and kissed two players.

Morganna's lawyer went on to explain that his client frequently suffered from this problem. 'Seven out of ten times if you lean her over a rail she topples over it. Anyone who knows anything about the law of gravity will understand that. You can't interfere with nature.'

After the judge had spent some time in his chambers discussing points of law and physics with the defendant, the case was dismissed.

LEGAL ISSUE, *Most Sensitive*

Reporting on a case of assaulting a policeman while in pursuit of his duty, the *Braintree and Witham Times* recently noted:

'The magistrates heard that a "fierce struggle" ensued during which the constable's testicles were grabbed and squeezed. . . . Fining him £30 or 40 days in prison, Chairman of the Justices, Mr Alfred Playle, told him he should not take the law into his own hands.'

LITERARY BONKS,

Ten Least Well-Known

ONE

Wednesday 21 January 1801.
I dined at Deane yesterday, as I told you I should; — & met the two Mr Holdens. — We played at Vingt-un, which as Fulwar was unsuccessful, gave him an opportunity of exposing himself as usual.

Jane Austen, in a letter to her sister Cassandra

TWO

Stop a minute; let those two people go on, or I shall have to speak to them. I do detest conventional intercourse. Nasty! They are going into the church, too. Oh, the Britisher abroad!

E.M. Forster, *A Room with a View*

THREE

She touched his organ, and from that bright epoch, even it, the old companion of his happiest hours, incapable as he had thought of elevation, began a new and deified existence.

Charles Dickens, *Martin Chuzzlewit*

An illustration of Darwinism. Without use, an organ dwindles; with use, it increases. For instance, the organ of a grinder who, in the struggle for existence, relies entirely on his instrument, is invariably larger than that of the grinder who, in addition, uses a monkey. Most of our readers must have noticed this.

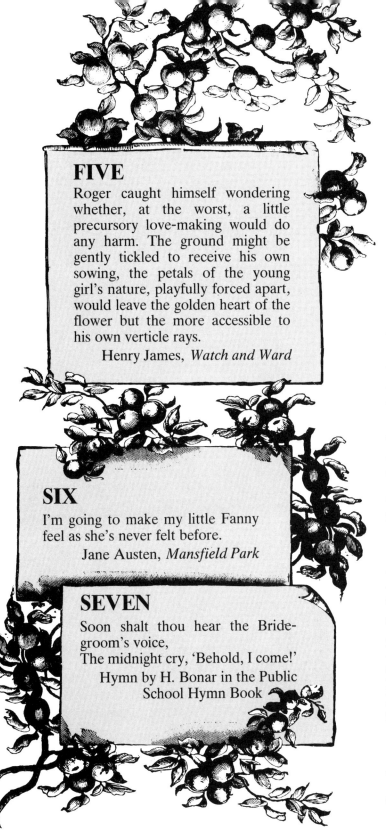

FIVE

Roger caught himself wondering whether, at the worst, a little precursory love-making would do any harm. The ground might be gently tickled to receive his own sowing, the petals of the young girl's nature, playfully forced apart, would leave the golden heart of the flower but the more accessible to his own verticle rays.

Henry James, *Watch and Ward*

SIX

I'm going to make my little Fanny feel as she's never felt before.

Jane Austen, *Mansfield Park*

SEVEN

Soon shalt thou hear the Bridegroom's voice,
The midnight cry, 'Behold, I come!'

Hymn by H. Bonar in the Public School Hymn Book

EIGHT

'It makes me feel very queer,' he said; 'it makes me feel — queer.'

The Earl looked at the boy in silence. It made him feel queer too — queerer than he had ever felt in his whole life. And he felt more queer still when he saw there was a terrible expression on the small face which was usually so happy. . . .

'Shall I be your boy, even if I'm not going to be an earl?' And his flushed little face was all alight with eagerness. How the old Earl did look at him from head to foot, to be sure! How his great shaggy brows did draw themselves together, and how queerly his deep eyes shone under them — how very queerly!

'My boy!' he said . . . 'Yes, you'll be my boy as long as I live; and, by George, sometimes I feel as if you were the only boy I ever had.'

Cedric's face turned red to the roots of his hair.

Frances Hodgson Burnett,
Little Lord Fauntleroy

NINE

'You young men who like kissing and laughter
And who follow a life that is gay;
Don't forget you must pay for it after;
I can show you a much better way,
For I'm going to get married today.'

Edward J. Dent's translation of
Mozart's *Don Giovanni*

TEN

'I rather fancy her dead.'

Mrs Gaskell, *North and South*

LIVE SHOW, *Least Erotic*

'It was a convention of the sexual revolution but it was the most sexless event imaginable,' said Craig Sams, a delegate to the famous Wet Dream festival, which was held in Amsterdam in November 1970.

Sams has particularly vivid memories of the much-publicized last night of the festival when the legendary Dutch sexual revolutionary Otto Muhl was due to put on a bad taste spectacular, involving the sexual abuse and sacrifice of a live animal.

At first Muhl and his followers merely leapt about the stage, stark naked to the sound of the Rolling Stones. Then, at the climax of the show, a sedated goose was brought on to the stage and a knife produced.

Unfortunately the prospect of watching a bird being raped and then decapitated failed to appeal to some members of the audience. The English writer Heathcote Williams leapt out of his seat, brought Otto down with a classic rugby tackle, grabbed the goose and passed it to someone in the front row who made off with it.

According to Sams, 'Otto and his team had a tantrum on stage, continued to dance around shaking their fists at the audience and eventually crapped on the stage and went off.'

An alternative sex object

LOBBYIST, *Hardest Working*

Even in a city known for its scandals, the confessions of Paula Parkinson, one of Washington's leading political lobbyists, caused something of a stir in 1981.

Commenting on her holiday spent alone in a cottage with three Republican congressmen (who included one T. Dan Quayle), Mrs Parkinson expressed surprise that anyone was shocked. Over the past three years, she had slept with 'less than a dozen' congressmen in the course of her work. Almost all of them were Republicans and several were supporters of the Moral Majority. She had had sex with three congressmen in their offices, one in the garage of his office building, and used to send assignation notes to another on the floor of the House.

Among those in the know, a relationship with Paula was described as 'Parkinson's disease' because 'it really makes your hand shake.' Interviewed by the national press, the lobbyist's husband managed to claim some of the credit by apologizing to the nation for having created what he called 'a sexual Frankenstein.'

Paula Parkinson resigned as a lobbyist later in 1981 on a matter of principle. Following an all-night party she had thrown for a few friends, several congressmen were so hung over the next day that they were unable to vote on a bill to bail out the Chrysler motor company. 'Here was a bill that would affect millions and millions of lives,' she said, 'and these congressmen were using their power to get laid, not get votes. . . . My morals might be low, but at least I have principles.'

# LOVE-MAKERS, *Most Talkative*
>>> **WORK**, *Sexologist Most Frequently Interrupted while at.*

LOVE, *Most Broad-Minded Definition of*

Starlet Viviane Ventura has some words of warning for those tempted by the idea of sex without commitment. 'You should always be in love with the man you're sleeping with,' she says, adding helpfully, 'it doesn't matter if your love only lasts two minutes.'

M<u>ALE HYSTERIA</u>, *Most Excusable Cases of*

One of the most powerfully matriarchal communities in the world is the Tchambuli tribe in New Guinea. There the men are considered pointless, inferior beings, fit only for breeding, and are kept apart from the women except when strictly necessary.

According to anthropologists, male Tchambulis are subject to frequent outbursts of hysterical insecurity.

M<u>ARITAL AID</u>, *Oddest*

After his second marriage, the critic Kenneth Tynan temporarily gave up his love of discipline (>>> **SPANKER**, *Most Serious-Minded*) for more conventional pleasures. All the same, certain intimate problems remained.

'Our first declared confrontation was over sex,' wrote Kathleen Tynan, his wife and later his biographer. 'As part of my new-broom policy at Mount Street, I systematically invaded cupboards and drawers throwing out old make-up bottles, other women's clothes, and objects that could only have been there for sexual use: a cork on a long string attached to a hot-water bottle, a pair of Victorian knickers and a single black stocking.'

She declined to explain quite how the cork, string and hot-water bottle were employed.

>>> **HIGH-BROW PORNOGRAPHY**, *Least Successful Work of*, **GOING SOLO: THE GOOD AND THE BAD NEWS SUPPLEMENT**.

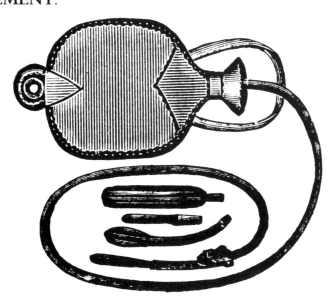

MATING RITUALS, *Ten Least Romantic*

ONE

During the punk revolution of the late 1970s, the British press were particularly interested in the sexual habits of the new rebels. One punk explained precisely how contact was established: 'When you fancy a girl, you spit in each other's glasses, then the boy punk says, "Do you?", the girl answers "Yes", and you go up to the toilets.'

TWO

One of the less well-known achievements of the celebrated poet Rupert Brooke was that he persuaded Virginia Woolf to bathe nude with him when she stayed in Grantchester in 1909.

There, it's believed likely that the great novelist was subjected to Brooke's favourite party trick — jumping into a pond called Byron's Pool to emerge, seconds later, with a fully fledged erection.

Virginia Woolf's comments on this behaviour are not on record.

THREE

Punch's 'Country Life' column reported the following incident from the *Reading Evening Post*:

'A mystery man on a bicycle is being sought by police following two incidents in which Reading women have been jabbed in the buttocks. The police have been told that a man rode up behind young women in the town, stuck what is believed to be a school compass into them, and rode off.'

FOUR

Addressing himself to a group of adoring girl fans, sixties rock idol Jim Morrison opted for the direct approach. 'You're all a bunch of fucking idiots,' he said. 'Your faces are being pressed into the shit of the world. Take your fucking friend and love him. Do you want to see my cock?'

FIVE

'The worst lay in the world,' is the way Peter Lawford described Rita Hayworth, with whom he once had a brief affair. 'She was always drunk and she was always eating.' According to Lawford, the legendary sex goddess used to get up as soon as they had made love, go to the kitchen, sit on the floor and eat everything she could find in the fridge. For Rita, sex was at best foreplay to a massive pig-out.

She eventually found the ideal partner for a beautiful kitchen-based romance — Orson Welles.

SIX

The whores in Kabul are famous for their sense of humour, particularly at the expense of foreigners.

A favourite trick is for a girl to lure her victim into a house off the street where she and her colleagues work (known helpfully as the Street of Fornication), tease him with slaps and tickles, playfully apply dark red make-up to his face, undress him and make him stand naked in the bedroom while she and her 'mother' (the madam) pelt him with feather cushions.

As this exotic foreplay reaches its climax, the girl starts to slip out of her clothes and runs from the room, challenging the punter to catch her. He pursues her, with growing excitement, through the house. Just as he's about to catch her, she slips through a curtain — which leads straight back out on to the Street of Fornication.

There the local people are used to seeing naked, sexually aroused, heavily made-up foreigners standing in confusion on the pavement — they mock him as a catamite, beat him and sexually assault him until he is finally arrested for indecency by the local police.

SEVEN

In his journal of 1st August 1801, the author Stendhal contained a helpful step-by-step guide to the method of seduction most popular among Frenchmen:

'Like many others, I'm embarrassed when it comes to _____ a respectable woman for the first time. Here's a very simple method. While she's laying down, you start kissing her lightly, you titillate her, etc., she begins to like it. Still, through force of habit, she keeps defending herself. Then, without her realizing what you're up to, you should put your left forearm on her throat, beneath her chin, as if you are going to strangle her. Her first movement will be to raise her hand in defence. Meanwhile you take your _____ between the index and middle finger of your right hand, holding them both taut, and quietly place it in the _____ . . . . It's important to cover up the decisive movement of the left forearm by whimpering.'

EIGHT

In Anglo-Saxon times, Danish soldiers were notorious for their cruelty and rapaciousness. On seeing a shipload of raiders from the convent wall, the English abbess, Ebbe, ordered all the nuns in her charge to cut off their noses and upper lip in the hope of discouraging the Danes. It failed — all of them were deflowered, including the abbess.

NINE

'She tried to pull me once,' boasts hippie photographer Keith Morris in describing his relationship during the sixties with Germaine Greer. He had come to know her rather well, having been chosen by her to take exceedingly graphic portraits of her private parts for the magazine *Suck* ('a pretty revolting experience,' he claims). 'Her thing was to hang from my minstrel gallery and swing like some great bat, while murmuring sexy things at me. This was supposed to turn me on but the effect it actually had was to make me run upstairs and lock the darkroom door. . . . These were very big ladies. It made me feel inadequate.'

TEN

'The English had a curious habit of fucking on foot, fully clothed,' an American GI stationed in Britain during the war later recalled. The habit was particularly popular with whores in London — the so-called 'Piccadilly Warriors' — who used to yell out to passing GIs, 'Hey, Yank, want it quick Marble Arch style?'

The reason for the popularity of the Marble Arch position was that many of the girls believed that being vertical avoided the risk of pregnancy.

Germaine: made Keith feel inadequate

MELBOURNE, *Lord*

>>> **GOVERNMENT**, *Strongest Believer in the Smack of Firm.*

MILLIONAIRESS, *Straightest*

'There are times when I like sex and times when I don't,' Barbara Hutton told an interviewer. 'When I'm in the mood for it, I like nothing better. But I don't enjoy cruelty. I hate it when somebody I don't know comes out wearing a rubber diving suit with a battleship in one hand and a jar of vaseline in the other.'

MIRACLE, *Most Embarrassing*

It was the custom of the Archbishop of Cologne in the late fifteenth century to allow his jester to sleep at the foot of his bed. One night, the jester awoke to find more feet than usual obtruding from the end of the bed.

'Whose foot is this?' he asked, grabbing one of them.

'Mine,' said the Archbishop.

'And this? And this? And this?'

'Mine,' the Archbishop said each time.

The Fool leapt up and ran to the door. 'A miracle!' he shouted at the top of his voice. 'A miracle!' He ran down the corridor crying, 'Come quickly! The Archbishop has grown four legs.'

As the prelate's retinue gathered around his bed, a naked nun was discovered behind the arras.

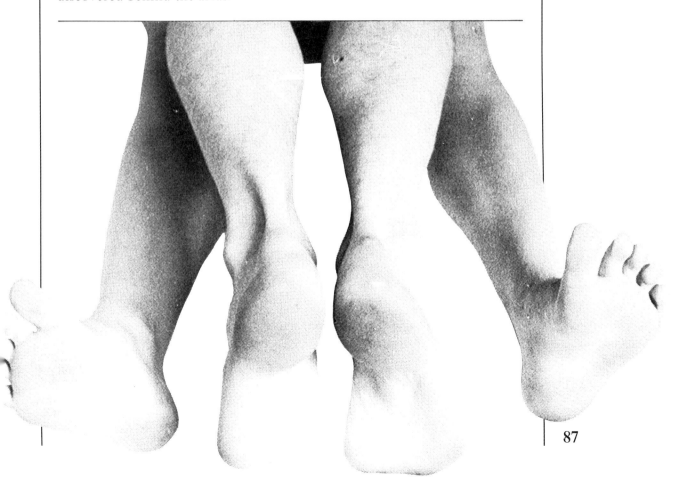

MISSILE, *Least Memorable*

A middle-aged man's attempt to make a direct political statement by exposing himself to peace women protesting at Greenham Common backfired badly when the women gathered round to jeer and laugh at him. The flasher fled.

'The women didn't even bother reporting it,' commented a local police spokesman. 'They obviously considered it such a small thing that it wasn't worth talking about.'

MISSIONARY, *Most Easily Traumatized*

The Reverend Harris, a middle-aged missionary during Victorian times, found that bringing the word of God to heathens involved unusual problems. Visiting the island of Marquesas, he found that the inhabitants were friendly but appeared to view him with some distrust, particularly after he persistently refused to accept their traditional offering to visitors, sexual intercourse with the tribal chief's wife.

It was rumoured among the Marquesans that Harris was some kind of supernatural being without the needs of normal human beings. Out of curiosity, two women of the tribe crept into his tent as he slept, with the intention of discovering whether the strange white man actually possessed a male member. Harris awoke to find two native women rummaging about eagerly in his pyjamas.

Fleeing the encampment that night, he was found the next day by the crew of his ship, wandering on the beach, according to reports, 'in a lamentable condition, like a man who had lost his reason'.

He left the island that day, never to return.

MONARCH, *Unhappiest*

From the moment they were married, the Prince of Wales (later George IV) and his bride Princess Caroline of Brunswick were united only by mutual distaste for one another. On first meeting her, George backed away, turned to a friend and said faintly, 'Harris, I am not well, pray get me a glass of brandy.' In her turn Caroline confided to the Earl of Malmesbury that she found the Prince extremely fat and not nearly as handsome as his portraits. Rather pathetically, she asked if he was always as ugly as that.

At their wedding ceremony, the Prince was so drunk that he was scarcely able to stand. Later, when he was finally obliged to join his wife in the bridal chamber, he tumbled into the fireplace where he spent the night.

The relationship did not improve with time. George first moved into a different wing of the palace to escape her 'personal nastiness'. When this proved inadequate, he threw her out altogether, In retaliation, Caroline went on a wild binge of promiscuity and partying, pretended to have had an illegitimate child and, during a tour of Europe, enjoyed a much publicized fling with an Italian gigolo.

Years later, one of the king's ministers hurried to him with news of Napoleon's death.

'Sire,' he said, 'your greatest enemy is dead.'

'Is she, by God?' said the king.

Princess Caroline enjoys a relaxed moment with a young admirer

89

MONROE, *Marilyn*

>>> FREUDIAN, *Least Successful* and QUOTATIONS, *Five Least Romantic.*

MORRISON, *Jim*

>>> MATING RITUALS, *Ten Least Romantic.*

MULTIPLE ORGASM, *Least Enjoyable*

Religious worship in an exclusive Irani sect, into which only beautiful youths are admitted, can be an arduous and messy business.

The adherents, whose god is the sun-god Mithras, are required to sit naked in the blazing sun. At midday, it's ordained that they become sexually aroused and cast their semen towards the sun — without touching themselves. This performance must be repeated three times, after which the worshippers invariably collapse.

Failure to worship the god in this way results in immediate expulsion and disgrace.

She gave great nose

NASAL SEX, *Most Publicized Case of*

Among the revelations Fiona Wright, Queen of the Bimbos, made about Sir Ralph Halpern, there was one intimate detail that was more plausible than his five-times-a-night achievements, or even his claim to have goosed Mrs Thatcher at Downing Street.

Sir Ralph, according to his ex-lover, was particularly sensitive about the size of his nose. After they had made love, he would require Fiona to stroke it gently and make loving, reassuring remarks about it.

>>> **STATISTICAL APPENDIX**.

NATIONAL HERO, *Least Dignified*

According to Aubrey's *Brief Lives*, Sir Walter Raleigh had a somewhat tetchy relationship with his son, who was also called Walter.

On one occasion, the great Englishman was obliged to take his son to an official dinner. Having been warned to be on his best behaviour, the young man 'sate next to his Father and was very demure at leaste halfe dinner time.'

Then, to the consternation of the other guests, he announced that he had visited a whore that morning. 'I was very eager of her, kissed and embraced her, and went to enjoy her,' he said, 'but she thrust me from her and vowed I should not, *For your father lay with me but an hower ago.*'

Enraged and embarrassed, Raleigh struck his son a great blow in the face. Aware that brawling in public with national heroes was a serious breach of etiquette, Walter responded by hitting the guest next to him as hard as he could.

'Box about,' he cried. 'Twill come to my Father anon.'

NEIGHBOUR, *Busiest*

'It's a miracle he's ever fathered one kid, never mind five,' commented Miss Doreen Staples, after her former lover had been revealed as a 'Council-house Casanova' in the local paper. The man, it had been revealed, was the father of five different children by three women who live on the same estate. 'He's a total waste of bed space,' added Miss Staples who is the mother of two of Casanova's children.

The man's active lifestyle first came to the attention of the press when he used to run through the estate singing, to the tune of the famous TV soap, 'Neighbours, I've been having all my neigbours.'

NERVOUS BREAKDOWN, *Messiest*

'I've noticed it before,' recalled Nell Kimball, who was a madam in New Orleans during World War I, 'the way the idea of a war and dying makes a man raunchy, and wanting to have it as much as he could. It wasn't really a pleasure at times but a kind of nervous breakdown that could only be treated with a girl and a set-to.'

NOVELIST, *Silliest*

While travelling through Italy with his wife, the novelist Bulwer Lytton would frequently embarrass her by wearing extravagant and ludicrous costumes.

On one occasion, the couple were riding in an open carriage when an attractive young girl, standing in the doorway of a cottage, stared at them as they passed.

'Did you notice how that girl looked at me?' the novelist asked his wife smugly.

Lady Lytton was unimpressed. 'If you wear that ridiculous dress, no wonder people stare at you,' she replied.

Lytton was so enraged by this response that he set out to prove her wrong. 'You think that people stare at my dress; and not at me: I will give you the most absolute and convincing proof that your theory has no foundation,' he cried, stripping off his clothes.

The novelist then rode on the carriage for ten miles, naked except for his hat and boots, and proved his case to his own satisfaction, if not his wife's.

NUDIST CAMPAIGN, *Least Successful*

Despite an extensive publicity campaign, attempts by a group of nudists on the Japanese island of Fujishima to establish their own political party have proved unsuccessful. At the first annual convention of the Japanese Sauna Party, whose slogan was 'The Rotary Club for the Naked', fewer than two dozen enthusiasts appeared, wearing flesh-coloured tights.

NYMPHOMANIACS, *Worst News for*

In his frank and probing study *The Frustrated Woman* (a 'revealing report intended to contribute to our understanding and compassion for the frustrated female'), Dr Karl U. Hansen warns that the disease of nymphomania is reaching epidemic proportions. Published in 1959, the report blames what he calls the sexual revolution of the twentieth century and points out that 'uncounted women simply aren't bothering to wear underclothes at all now'. As a result, many young women grow up to be at least 'semi-nymphomaniacs'.

In a series of probing chapters in the book, covering such topics as 'The girl who loved being spanked', 'Alcohol and the over-sexed woman' and 'Are call-girls Nymphos?', we discover that the average frustrated woman is liable to have a dominant mother, a fondness for drink, and lesbian tendencies. She is generally uninterested in foreplay. 'I'm annoyed with the men who think I want a lot of playing around before we get to it,' explained one of Dr Hansen's patients, Dorothy W. 'Maybe some girls like to have men fiddle, but to me it's a complete waste of time.' The average nymphomaniac rarely experiences orgasm.

In a reassuring final word, the doctor has better news for the husband who reads his book and says to himself, 'But that's a description of my wife'. I'll bet she's neurotically ill. I'll bet she's a nymphomaniac.'

Not necessarily true, according to Dr Hansen. 'Many women are highly sexed, yet frequently do not reach a climax in their sex relations. This does *not* necessarily mean they are nymphomaniacs.

# O'CONNOR, *Des*
>>> **WEDDING DAYS**, *Five Worst.*

OFFENSIVE WEAPON,
Most Effective Use of Underwear as an

'I have sentenced you to hell,' Mrs Jean Cassidy, a thirty-one-year-old mother of three children, wrote to a local detective inspector. While the note was something of an exaggeration, Mrs Cassidy certainly made life difficult for the policeman, for whom she had developed a powerful obsession.

She threw a brick through his car window, made false 999 calls to his home, sent a black sympathy card to his wife which read 'Sorry about Frank' and tried to stab another policeman. Finally she stuffed a pink bra into the petrol tank of his car and set light to it.

Sentencing Mrs Cassidy to a year in jail for arson, damage, assault and possession of an offensive weapon, a local magistrate pointed out that her behaviour was particularly serious in view of the fact that she had only just been released from prison for committing similar offences in the past.

OLD BOOZER WITH A LOW SPERM COUNT, *Silliest*

Retired hellraiser and actor Oliver Reed has firm, if predictable, views about women. 'I like them in their place,' he once told a journalist in an exclusive interview. 'I like them on their knees, in the kitchen, doing the dusting.'

The good news for those wishing to become involved with the old charmer was that this is not an entirely one-sided arrangement. 'In return,' he pointed out reasonably, 'I feed them, wine them, make them laugh occasionally — and give them a punch on the nose and a good kicking when they need it. They're happier that way. They feel secure.'

Despite this intimate knowledge of what women want, Reed was often disappointed by their basic lack of imagination. 'You can't tell your girl or wife that going to bed with someone else is just like going to the lav and bears no relevance to fidelity. They are more emotional, they get uptight, close doors, change locks and talk to solicitors.'

Sadly, the loveable rogue's bedroom activities proved to be a more complex business than going to the lav. Years later, in another exclusive, he confided to the *News of the World* that he was unable to have a child with his young wife. 'I'm too old,' he said. 'I'm worn out. I've run out of sperm.'

Good old Olly: a low sporran count

Sir Thomas conducts a solo

OPENING FOR A SERMON,
Least Convincing

>>> EXCUSES, *Fifteen Weakest*.

OPERATIC PERFORMANCE,
Most Misunderstood

Anxious to enlist the services of the famous German soprano Martha Fuchs for a Covent Garden production of Tosca, Sir Thomas Beecham sent a talent scout to Berlin to hear her sing.

He soon received a telegram from Germany with his colleague's considered verdict. 'MARTHA FUCKS WONDERFUL', it read.

'I'M SURE SHE DOES AND I'M GLAD YOU'RE BOTH ENJOYING YOURSELF', went Beecham's inevitable reply, 'BUT CAN SHE SING TOSCA?'

ORACLE, *Worst News from the*

Asked by Roman worshippers what they should do to make their Sabine women, many of whom were sterile, bear children, the great oracle spoke from the sacred forest of Mount Esquith. It said, 'Let the women be impregnated by a goat.'

No thanks, Billy

Since they were going through one of their rare fastidious phases, the Romans elected to interpret this by ordering a great ceremony at which all sterile men and women should walk naked, flogging each other with thongs made from goatskin.

This is one of the earliest recorded instances of mass flagellation.

ORAL SEX, *Least Satisfying Act of*

Fun-loving grandfather Arthur Brown responded gamely when his birthday treat — a kissogram girl dressed only in balloons — made a surprise entry at his party. Dropping to his knees, he attempted to bite the balloons off with his teeth. Unfortunately he dislocated his jaw.

'I just had to put up with the pain,' he commented later. 'I burst the rest with my hands until I could go to hospital.'

ORAL SEX, *Weakest Case Against*

In their book *Intended for Pleasure*, authors Dr Ed and Gaye Wheat argue that all Christian couples should avoid the temptation of oral-genital sex which, they say, 'some already find repugnant.'

The reason for this is that 'oral-genital sex definitely limits the amount of loving, verbal communication that husband and wife may have as they make love.'

ORGASM, *Three Least Helpful Remarks about the*

According to the lesson of the laboratory there is only one perfect orgasm . . . the orgasm achieved on one's own. Nor should we be surprised if such solitary pleasure becomes the ideal by which all mutual sex is measured.

Dr Leslie H. Farber

Sex has become the religion of the most civilized portions of the earth. The orgasm has replaced the Cross as the focus of longing and the image of fulfilment.

Malcolm Muggeridge

In the case of some women, orgasms take quite a bit of time. Before signing on with such a partner, make sure you are willing to lay aside, say, the month of June, with sandwiches having to be brought in.

Bruce Jay Friedman

'ORRIBLE SIGHT, *Most*

There's nothing new about lovers becoming inextricably attached while making love. A fourteenth-century English knight records a case where this painful medical condition was put down to divine intervention:

'It happened that one Pres Lenard, a sergeant on the night delt flesshely with a woman in church. By a miracle they were tyes fast togedre that night and the morwe alle day. People came to see the miracle and all prayed that orrible sight might be ended. So the offenders were separated. And they that dede the dede were ioyned to penaunce to go naked afore the procession three Sondays beting them self and recordying her synne before the pepille.'

# OSBORNE, *John*
>>> CONDOM CORNER.

OTHER SIDE, *Most Surprising News from the*

According to a story told in Philip Toynbee's *End of a Journey*, a friend of Jessica Mitford was anxious to reach her husband who had recently died. She visited a spiritualist who, to her surprise, made contact.

'What is it like there?' the woman asked.

The spiritualist moaned and, in a strange voice, said, 'Oh we run about a bit, eat, have a lot of sex, run about a bit more.'

'But, dear, I didn't know Heaven was like that.'

'Oh, I'm not in Heaven,' came the reply. 'I'm a rabbit in Australia.'

PAPAL VISIT, *Unholiest*

The eight-year stay of Pope Innocent IV and his entourage in the French town of Lyons during the fourteenth century had some unexpected side-effects. 'Since we came here we have effected great improvements,' said Cardinal Hugo in a farewell address to the townspeople. 'When we came we found but three or four brothels. We leave behind us only one,' he said. 'We must add, however, that it extends from the eastern to the western gate.'

An incubus: mostly hot air

98

PARANORMAL EXPERIENCE,
Least Rewarding

Among the many works of the devil discovered by the Inquisition during the Middle Ages was the frequent appearance of evil male spirits, known as Incubi, who used to seduce women and turn them into deluded witches.

'At times women also think they have been made pregnant by an Incubus,' one Inquisitor wrote, 'and their bellies grow to an enormous size; but when the time of parturition comes, their swelling is relieved by no more than the explosion of a great quantity of wind.'

PARATROOPER, *Most Aptly Named*

Captain Richard Head, an officer in the paratroop regiment, has been severely reprimanded by his commanding officer following a fracas in a night club. The incident occurred just after the comedian on stage had asked his name and, on being told it was Dick Head, had made certain disrespectful remarks. Screaming, 'I'm a para! I can knock you senseless!', Captain Head had to be restrained by other members of his party. He was later ejected from the club.

I can knock you senseless

PARTY POLITICAL BROADCAST, *Worst*

'I used to be Sergeant Norman Almodovar of the Bay Highway Patrol. Three years ago I changed sex and became a call girl,' explained the Libertarian candidate for Lieutenant Governor of California, Miss Norma Almodovar. 'I know there have been complaints about my poster which, as you see, shows me in a bikini and red boxing gloves striking a Rocky-10 type pose. I would have preferred to appear in the nude, of course, but to have done so would have been a violation of my probation order.'

PATRIOT, *Greediest*

A Canadian major stationed in England during the First World War was at first impressed by British standards of hospitality when a titled lady invited him for a weekend at her stately home. He was even more impressed when her ladyship explained over dinner that her husband had been killed at the front and that she regarded it as her patriotic duty to keep up the morale of those on leave. 'So,' she concluded unambiguously, 'here I am.'

The major needed no further encouragement and spent the night with her.

The next morning, he was taken aside by the butler.

'Her ladyship has the greatest difficulty maintaining this estate,' he said quietly. 'It would be most helpful if you would leave a contribution of a hundred pounds.'

PHILIP, *Prince*

>>> **ITEM OF PALACE REGALIA**, *Least Frequently Worn.*

POETIC LICENCE, *Saddest Case of*

The friends of Victorian poet Algernon Charles Swinburne had become increasingly concerned about the direction his sex life was taking and resolved to find someone to introduce him to the joys of heterosexual love.

The actress Adah Isaacs Menken was finally approached for this delicate task. Miss Isaacs Menken was appearing in a review, which involved her being led around the stage, dressed only in tights, strapped to the back of a horse. Although she was not pretty in the conventional sense, she had a good figure and, having been married several times, was thought to be ideally qualified.

Dante Gabriel Rossetti took Swinburne to see the show and confided in him that Miss Isaacs Menken harboured a passion for him. Reluctantly the poet agreed to meet her.

At first, all appeared to be going well. On their first meeting, the actress spent the night at Swinburne's lodgings and for several weeks she would visit him regularly.

Finally Miss Isaacs Menken threw in the towel. She told Rossetti that 'she didn't know what it was, but she hadn't been able to get him up to the scratch.' When pressed for details, she remarked dolefully, 'I can't make him understand that *biting*'s no use.'

PRESIDENTIAL BEHAVIOUR,
Least Appropriate

Following an official dinner in Calcutta in 1880, the former President of the United States, General Ulysses S. Grant, was reported to have behaved in a profligate and drunken way towards several female members of his party.

'He fumbled Mrs A.,' Lord Lytton, Viceroy of India, later wrote to a friend, 'kissed the shrieking Miss B., pinched the plump Mrs C. black and blue and ran at Miss D. with intent to ravish her.'

Finally, the General was physically restrained by a party of sailors and carried back to his ship. Finding his wife in the public saloon bar, 'this remarkable man satiated there and then his baffled lust on the unresisting body of his legitimate spouse and copiously vomited during the operation. If you have seen Mrs Grant,' concludes Lytton, 'you will not think this incredible.'

# PRICK, *Fastest*
>>> **MATING RITUALS**, *Top Ten Least Romantic*.

PROSTITUTION, *Least Reliable Sign of*

Dr de Venette's *The Mysteries of Conjugal Love Reveal'd*, which was published in 1707, contains some moderately good news for worried husbands:

'Fines'd and curl'd Hair in the amorous Parts, a moist and open Clink, absence of the membrane Hymen, shaggy and discoloured *Nymphae*, the interior Orifice of the Womb widened, and the Voice chang'd is no sufficient Evidence of a Woman's being a Prostitute.'

The author goes on to suggest that, despite this reassuring advice, a newly married wife who is not a virgin would be wise to take further precautions. He particularly recommends inserting two or three pellets of lamb's blood on the honeymoon night.

QUAYLE, *T. Dan*

>>> LOBBYIST, *Hardest Working.*

QUEEN'S REPRESENTATIVE, *Least Dignified*

'You are all very stupid people not to see the propriety of it all,' Lord Cornbury, Governor-General of New York told his Assembly in 1702, when questioned as to why he was wearing a hooped evening gown, elaborate head-dress and carrying a fan. 'In this place, and on this occasion, I represent a woman, and in all respects I ought to represent her as faithfully as I can.'

For a while, the colonial elders accepted this explanation for Cornbury's penchant for appearing at public functions in his wife's dresses. He was, after all, first cousin to Queen Anne and known to be something of an individualist. He liked to be called 'His High Mightiness'. At the banquet welcoming him to New York, he had delivered a speech praising the sensuous beauty of his wife's earlobes and had insisted that, one by one, the guests should touch them for themselves. On one occasion, a night watchman was surprised by a drunken woman who had crept up behind him and tickled him. It turned out to be the Governor-General.

Lady Cornbury was scarcely more conventional. She inaugurated a series of governmental balls, to which local aristocrats were invited and then charged for entry. After visiting the homes of local gentry, she would send round a carriage to collect articles of furniture and clothing which had taken her fancy.

After five years of rampant financial and sexual impropriety, Cornbury went too far, even for the long-suffering people of New York, by appearing at his wife's funeral in one of her evening gowns. After representations from the assemblies of New York and New Jersey, Queen Anne decreed that the fact that the Governor-General was her cousin 'Should not Protect him in Oppressing her Subjects.'

Deeply in debt, Cornbury was ejected from office and thrown into prison. On assuming in 1709 the estate and title of his father, the Earl of Clarendon, he was released and returned to England where his behaviour was regarded as perfectly normal.

It is believed that his brief but eventful tenure of office advanced the cause of American Independence by several years.

The Queen's queen at an official function

QUESTIONNAIRE, *Most Unusual*

Over a period of three years, Peter Gardella, religious instructor and author of the book *Innocent Ecstasy*, asked his students certain questions which he regarded as pertinent to his studies.

The results were as follows:

Are you a regular churchgoer? YES — 41%.

Do you believe in the virgin conception of Jesus Christ? YES — 71%.

Have you any experience of oral-genital sex? YES — 61%.

Mr Gardella does not draw any particular conclusion from this survey.

QUOTATIONS, *Ten Least Romantic*

ONE

There's no such thing as romantic love. Every normally constituted young man wants to pop into bed with every normally constituted young woman. And vice versa. That's all there is to it.

H.G. Wells

TWO

Generally speaking, it is in love as it is in war, where the longest weapon carries it.

John Leland, *Fanny Hill*

THREE

Michael is not interested in girls and sex. He is definitely still a virgin and doesn't believe he has missed anything.

Chris Telvitt, Michael Jackson's Tour Manager

FOUR

This thing called love, there's none of it, you know, it's only fucking. That's all there is — just fucking.

James Joyce

FIVE

How is it that woman, who is soul-less herself, can discern the soul in man? How can she judge about his morality who is herself non-moral? How can she grasp his character when she has no character herself?

Otto Weinger, *Sex and Character*

SIX

One of the most painful and horrible things that one comes across in these days are the dreadful traits one finds in the female.

Mr Justice Humphreys

SEVEN

Love is a pretty kind of sporting fray, a thing will soon away; it is also a tooth-ache or like pain; a game where none doth gain.

Sir Walter Raleigh

EIGHT

An act which on sober reflection one recalls with repugnance, and in a more elevated mood even with disgust.

Schopenhauer

NINE

The public insists on its fantasies of Hollywood. Marilyn Monroe, on the screen, is the sexiest woman in the world. In real life she was blah. And always late.

Kirk Douglas

TEN

He that get a wench with child and marry her afterwards is as if a man should shit in his hat and then clap it on his head.

Samuel Pepys, *Diary*

RECEPTION, *Least Decorous Wedding*

Historically, wedding ceremonies in Samoa were not always entirely joyous occasions. In the past, it was the tradition for the bridegroom to test his new bride's virginity by the solemn, public insertion of two fingers. He would then hold them up.

If they were covered in blood, the festivities would begin; if not, the bride was clubbed to death by the wedding guests.

REED, *Oliver*

>>> OLD BOOZER WITH A LOW SPERM COUNT, *Silliest.*

REFORMED CHARACTER,
Most Dubiously

Discharged from a mental hospital in 1985, having spent four years there for killing a woman, Mr Issei Sagawa told reporters that he was fully cured. The thing to be most careful of in future relationships with women was not to eat them.

RELIGIOUS WORSHIP, *The Two Most*
Frequently Revered Objects of

Of the many different religious sects flourishing on the Indian sub-continent, there are two of particular interest.

The first, which is to be found in Bengal and parts of southern India, requires its young men to meditate for many hours every day and contemplate the Yoni, or female sex organ. Such is the intensity of their devotion that true adepts have been known to believe finally that they have actually become Yoni. As recently as thirty years ago, there were reports of religious ceremonies at which one woman was worshipped orgiastically by the entire male congregation.

The second sect is situated in the state of Madya Pradesh. In his book *A Short History of Sex-Worship*, H. Cutner describes their form of worship:

'When the priests leave their temples, they march out quite nude, ringing a bell. This brings all the women in the neighbourhood to the scene, and they profit by the occasion to worship Siva by kissing the sexual organs of the holy man. This devotion is expected to be received without any sign of emotion, under pain of punishment.'

The two sects are not thought to have discussed any form of religious exchange scheme.

REUNION, *Least Affectionate*

'What a way to start a marriage,' railway clerk Chris Rodway announced to the world's press.

Rodway had been waiting at Manchester airport for his Chinese bride Juan Wang, who had previously been prevented from joining her British husband by the Chinese authorities.

Unfortunately, Juan proved to be less interested in publicity than her husband. When she arrived at the airport, she was disguised as a man and completely ignored him.

'I'll be teaching her some English words she's never heard before,' Chris told the bemused journalists.

Mrs Rodway in her brilliant disguise

ROMANTIC GESTURE, *Most Pointless*

Elegant but mean-spirited, the nineteenth-century courtesan Thérèse La Paiva was said to have ruined many of her suitors with her greed and cruelty.

One young nobleman became so obsessed with her that he dissipated his fortune in his pursuit of her. One day he tearfully announced that he was down to his last 10,000 francs.

'Very well,' said Thérèse, apparently in a mood of playful generosity, 'bring them to me tomorrow. We'll set fire to them, and I'll be yours until the flames die out.'

The idiotic nobleman did what he was told. The next day he visited her flat, where she was waiting in a loose gown. She took the money, dropped them into a silver bowl, set light to them and threw her gown open to them. Unfortunately the man was so aghast at the sight of what was left of his fortune going up in smoke, that he stood there, slack-jawed and unable to move.

10,000 francs burns quite quickly, he discovered. In a matter of moments, he was ejected from Thérèse's flat, a broken — and broke — man.

ROYAL AUDIENCE, *Frankest*

When the Prince of Wales, later to be Edward VI, made his royal progress through the brothels of Paris, he particularly asked to meet the legendary courtesan Giulia Beneni. On meeting the prince, Miss Beneni surprised the royal party by turning her back to him and lifting her skirts to the waist.

Berated by her host, the Duc de Gramont, she replied that she was merely obeying instructions.

'You told me to show him my best side,' she said.

ROYAL MISTRESS, *Most Lethal*

Although Nell Gwynn was used to her lover and patron Charles II taking other women, she was adept at ensuring that they rarely lasted long at court.

On one occasion, she was found brawling with the Duchess of Portsmouth — better known as 'Squintabella' on account of her unfortunate cross eyes. Nell quickly bettered Squintabella and, according to one source, 'taking up her Coats, she burnt with a Candle all the Hair off those Parts which Modesty obliges to Conceal.'

On another occasion, Nell, who had discovered that a rival had been invited to the king's bed, entertained the woman at a pre-coital dinner where she doctored her meal with 'Physical Ingredients'.

'The Effect thereof,' reported Alexander Smith in his *The School of Venus*, 'had such an Operation upon the Harlot, when the King was Caressing her in Bed with the amorous Sports of *Venus*, that a violent and sudden Loosness obliging her Ladyship to discharge her Artillery, she made the King, as well as her self, in a most lamentable Pickle.'

The woman was not invited back to the royal suite and soon afterwards left the court.

Royal Photographer,
Most Affectionate

There was considerable excitement in the art world following an auction report in the *Evening Standard* of July 16th, 1986 which read: 'A painting of a nude Mick Jagger, taken from the rear by Cecil Beaton, was sold by London auctioneers Bonham's yesterday for £1,050.'

Russian, *Most Restless*

According to the 1939 volume *How D'You Do?*, there were few countries in the world where it was easier to get a divorce than Russia. The decision was made by a people's court over which three magistrates, chosen by ballot, presided. One woman had managed to get divorced no less than twenty-eight times between the ages of nineteen and twenty-six.

On one question, however, Russian law was strict. It was illegal to get divorced on the same day that you were married.

Sadistic Practice, *Oddest*

The Indian sexologist Som Deva throws much-needed new light on the activities of the Marquis de Sade in his book *The Marching Eros*, which was published in 1983.

'Sade brushes the dust off the labia of women asphyxiated in the smoky cell of sex,' he writes.

ONE

9.30. THIS WEEK. In the second of a two-part report on the social implications of the spread of AIDS, Jonathan Dimbleby puts last week's findings to the Minister of Health responsible, Tony Newton.

Brighton Evening Argus

TWO

In the rush to make money out of safe sex, Jiffi Condoms have recently introduced a new sales gimmick — with every packet of Jiffi, buyers are given cards showing a position from the Kama Sutra.

Unfortunately, the promotion has already caused the firm legal problems. One girl claimed that she had dislocated a hip while attempting the position on one of the cards. 'We did give out a warning not to attempt the positions unless you have a full knowledge of yoga,' a Jiffi spokesman commented.

The matter has now been referred to the firm's solicitors.

THREE

Mr Ton Kempts, secretary of the Dutch Bee Keeper's League, is to issue a protest against the Dutch Government's anti-AIDS campaign. 'The Government has decided on a Birds and Bees theme,' he said. 'Several times a day they show a television cartoon in which a lustful looking bee flies from flower to flower while a voiceover says, "There is a disease that spreads through sex." At the end of the cartoon the bee drops down dead.

'We would like to make it quite clear that bees are not promiscuous. They do not carry AIDS. And they do not visit flowers for sex — but for nectar.'

'True Stories', *Private Eye*

Busy but not bonking

FOUR

Is Sex Safe Any More? In a world with AIDS, the facts of life can kill you. Find out what safe sex is — and how you can have it. All this week with Christine Lund.

Daily News TV Guide,
Los Angeles

FIVE

It took a Belgian court under a minute to empty after a defendant, Monsieur Georges Le Maise, had announced that he had AIDS. A policeman then told him, through a crack in the door, to drive himself to Vaalasted Prison in a police van.

On arriving at the prison, Le Maise was refused entry until a doctor had been called to examine him. Calling to him from a window in the gatehouse, the prison governor ordered the defendant to turn the van round and drive it to the city dump. The case was later dismissed.

SEX IN SCOTLAND – A SPECIAL SUPPLEMENT

A Fraserburgh woman slept with a knife under her pillow and admitted trying to stab her husband as he was sleeping. But she said this was to protect herself from attack by her husband who slept with three knives under his pillow.

Aberdeen Press and Journal

A man who spent the last eight years working with Franciscan monks punched a woman and hit another when they refused to kiss him on an Edinburgh–Glasgow train.

Glasgow Evening Times

'Few of them wished to proceed to further education. The girls were dreaming of boys and babies, and the boys of sheep and whisky.'

Glasgow Evening Times

An enraged customer burst into a London sex shop, carrying a vibrator in one hand and a gun in the other. Claiming that the vibrator had failed to satisfy his wife, the man forced the shop's woman assistant to hand over £50 from the till. He then threw the vibrator to the floor and ran off.

'We are looking for a blond-haired Scotsman with protruding, uneven teeth,' said a police spokesman.

The most frightening fact about AIDS is that it can be spread by normal sex between men and women. This is still rare in Scotland.

Scottish Sunday Mail

The full, romantic subtleties of male courtship in Scotland, where it's known as 'getting your bag off', are charmingly captured in Dave Robertson's poem 'I'm a gadgie':

'The fanny lap your patter up
They like when you're rough
And if you dinnae fuck them
There's other bits of stuff.
We take them to the bar
And get them steaming first
And if you dinnae get a bag off
You can always steal their purse.'

Following the eleventh incident of indecent exposure in three months, the town of Douce Dunblane was described by the *Stirling Observer* as 'the flashing capital of Central region'.

Asked to comment on the outbreak, Central's Chief Constable refused to be pushed into panic measures. 'I am not too concerned,' he said. 'It tends to fall off in winter.'

'Police who spent Saturday night and yesterday morning searching the rain-swept Carrick Hills, south of Ayr, for a girl in distress found eventually that she may have been a rabbit.'

Glasgow Herald

Sir Iain Moncrieffe of that Ilk was said to have a curiously direct way of dealing with the fair sex. On one occasion, he and his wife arrived at a friend's house in Edinburgh, with a large amount of luggage. 'Don't carry all that up,' he said, as his host struggled up the stairs with two heavy suitcases. 'Her ladyship will do it.'

Sir Iain's other claim to fame was that he was one of the few men to have owned up to asking Mrs Thatcher to go to bed with him. She declined.

SIXTIES, *Most Comprehensively Ignored Medical Advice of the*

Speaking in 1963, Dr Ernest Claxton, the assistant secretary of the British Medical Association, gave the following warning to his contemporaries: 'As a doctor, I can tell you that extra- and pre-marital intercourse is medically dangerous, morally degrading and nationally destructive.'

It is not thought that the doctor's words were too carefully heeded during the subsequent decade.

SPANKER, *Most Serious-Minded*

'Sex means spank and beautiful means bottom and always will,' wrote the critic Ken Tynan, whose enthusiasm for mild sado-masochism was well documented, particularly by himself.

Fortunately for Tynan, he soon found an ideal partner in Eileen Rabbinowitz, who was mildly masochistic by inclination. 'Chastise' was one of his very favourite words, he told her. He felt that it had 'a good Victorian ring of retribution' to it. Ideally, according to Tynan, a spank should be administered in the drawing-room of one's aunt.

While reviewing Robert Melville's book *Erotic Art in the West*, Tynan complained that not nearly enough attention had been paid to 'soft flagellation'. The article was most memorable for its unusual definition of humanism: the humanist, wrote Tynan, was 'someone who remembers the face of the people he spanks.'

>>> **MARITAL AID**, *Oddest* and **GOING SOLO: THE GOOD AND THE BAD NEWS SUPPLEMENT**.

SPOILS OF WAR, *Least Appreciated*

After the surrender of Tobruk in 1941, the manageress of the local brothel requested a meeting with the British commanding officer. Reluctantly, the colonel agreed.

When she arrived, the woman brought with her some of her girls and generously offered to put them at the disposal of the British army. Unfortunately, an observer recalls, the women were 'unattractive, powdered and blowsy all of them'.

For a moment, the Colonel frisked his moustache, as if considering the proposal. Then he barked at his translator, 'Tell them to take ten paces to the rear — immediately!'

The girls fell back in disarray.

'And tell them this,' the Colonel continued, 'that they stink.'

STREAKING, *Weakest Argument against*

'I find streaking morally wrong,' a local councillor told the correspondent from the *Kiddeminster Shuttle*. 'If the Good Lord had intended us to run around with no clothes on then I am sure we would all have been born stark naked.'

TABOOS, *Ten Least Reasonable*

The world traveller should bear in mind that the timing and nature of sexual indulgence are frequently subject to local conditions. Doing the wrong thing at the wrong moment with the wrong person can result in your stay being brought to a premature, embarrassing and sometimes painful end. The following should be avoided:

1

Doing it in the daytime, after a dream or with a woman whose husband has been killed by a python, crocodile or hyena (among the Zulus);

2

Doing it on the birthday of the gods (China);

3

Doing it indoors (Papua New Guinea);

4

Doing it out of doors (among the Mayan Indians);

5

Sodomy, for which you can be sent to prison for life (the Isle of Man);

6

Doing it during a thunderstorm (parts of Africa);

7

Doing it with a grandparent, particularly if you're a grandparent yourself (Taiwan);

8

Doing it after planting a narcotic plant (among the Ivaro Indians);

9

Doing it with a nun, monk, member of your immediate family, or the family pet (western societies);

10

Doing it and then bathing in the ocean afterwards (among the Yapese islanders).

TECHNIQUE, *Least Effective Seduction*

'His mode hath bin dayly & in evening time when he had any opportunity to come into my father's house and trie to kiss mee; & get mee into his lap, & put his hand under my apron & further if he could,' said Elizabeth Holmes, aged nineteen, who was pursuing a legal complaint against Thomas Langhorne, town drummer of Cambridge, Massachusetts, on 6th November, 1663. She went on to testify in court that Langhorne used to 'tell filthy things that are too much and too troublesome to mention them.'

Pressed by the court to be rather more explicit, Miss Holmes revealed some of the filthy things in detail.

'Hee said a man with a long member was most pleasure to a woman, when it went home to the womb & if the foreskin slipt back two or three inches it would hurt her a little at first,' she said. 'Hee asked me if I had ever seen his slip back, for hee said that his would often slip back, & hee would often come in & sit down & his members would hang out & many strange words he would call them, & and if any body came in Hee would cast one leg over the other & hide them. . . . He said he would lye with his wife three or four times in the night & when he had done it it would bee as limber as a rag &

that it would be two member entered wives body, & showed me as it in the acting of it. hand to my belly, & storeys he told mee & from honest men

hours in filling, also that his three handfulles into his measured a stick & grew bigger & longer One time Hee got his he said that most of the Hee had out of Aristotle & women'.

The court twenty-one Miss Holmes familiarity' future.

sentenced Langhorne to lashes and warned to avoid 'bold in the

TEDDY, *Most Over-Publicized*

The affection of the late Poet Laureate John Betjeman for his teddy bear Archie is well-known. Throughout his life, they were always together and frequently Betjeman would surprise strangers by conducting conversations with his love-object. On one occasion, while travelling on the London underground with Archie on his lap, he whispered loudly in the bear's ear, 'See that couple over there? They're looking at you. Behave.'

Less well-documented is the fact that Archie played an important role in Betjeman's marriage. During marital arguments, Lady Betjeman would threaten the bear with mortal injury, even going so far as holding it over a well until Betjeman capitulated. Distraught and tearful, the poet laureate admitted defeat.

Towards the end of his life, there were signs that Betjeman's relationship with Archie was not as idyllic as he had once thought. Asked by a BBC interviewer if he had any regrets, the poet answered, 'Yes. I wish I had had more sex.'

>>> **BOTTOM-WORSHIPPERS' HALL OF FAME**, *Top Five in the*.

TELEPHONE TART PHONE-INS,
Five Least Promising Titles for

1 *Washing Her Knickers.*

2 *In Arrears.*

3 *I Bonked a Housewife.*

4 *Used Undies.*

5 *Let Me Hold Your Balls.*

THATCHER, *Margaret*

>>> **ART CRITIC**, *Most Sex-Obsessed*, **NASAL SEX**, *Most Publicized Case of*, **SEX IN SCOTLAND – A SPECIAL SUPPLEMENT** and **VICTORIAN VALUES**, *Most Frequently Forgotten*.

THEATRICAL PARTICIPATION,
Most Extreme Case of

There were protests from the Friends of the Brewhouse Theatre after the management had agreed that a group of nudists should be allowed to enjoy the play *Steaming* stark naked.

'This is "in the raw" theatre,' said a spokesman for the theatre, defending the decision. 'There have been objections on moral grounds. But the main worry is hygiene. People fear AIDS. However, the nudists will be screened off from the rest of the audience and individual washable seat covers will be supplied.

It's all about bums on seats, darling

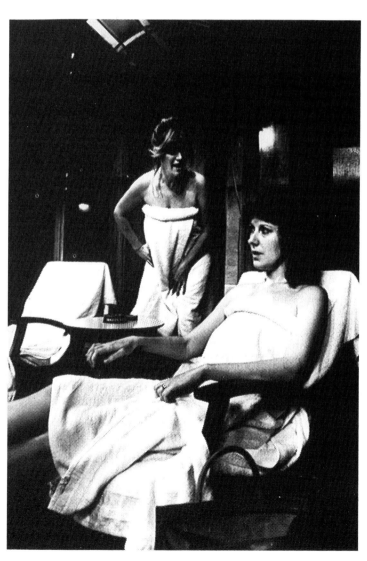

THURBER, *James*

>>> ESCORT, *Least Reliable.*

TRIBE, *Least Fun-Loving*

According to Margaret Mead, there is one aspect of the otherwise uninteresting Manus tribe, inhabitants of the Admiralty Islands, that is of particular interest to anthropologists and sexologists: they can't stand anything to do with sex. Manuan women are invariably frigid and their menfolk regard the business of conceiving children as a humiliating waste of time.

Kissing, fondling and foreplay are regarded as the height of bad behaviour among the tribe and its culture contains not one romantic song or story. There is no Manuan word for 'love'.

TYNAN, *Kenneth*

>>> BOTTOM-WORSHIPPERS' HALL OF FAME, *Top Five in the*, GOING SOLO: THE GOOD NEWS AND THE BAD NEWS SUPPLEMENT, HIGH-BROW PORNOGRAPHY, *Least Successful Work of*, MARITAL AID, *Oddest* and SPANKER, *Most Serious-Minded.*

UNDERGRADUATE FONDLER, *Least Satisfying*

Apart from hanging around Hugh Gaitskell and asking whether he could stroke his bottom (>>> BOTTOM-WORSHIPPERS' HALL OF FAME, *Top Five in the*), John Betjeman also spent much of his time at Oxford with W.H. Auden, with whom he once spent the night. Unfortunately, the loving couple were surprised in the morning by a Christ Church College 'scout' whose silence Auden bought for a fiver.

'It wasn't worth the £5,' he later grumbled to his friends.

UNHOLY WEDLOCK,

Five Most Depressing Reports On

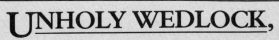

ONE

George Shamblin insisted he was trying to save his wife from drowning when he threw rocks at her as she struggled in the Kanawha River. 'I was trying to drive her back to shore,' he said.

Pittsburg Press

TWO

A Coventry housewife set fire to her husband's bedroom door in an attempt to save her marriage, Warwick Crown Court heard today. She had previously thrown paraffin at the door.

Coventry Evening Telegraph

THREE

CLIFF MADE LOVE TO MY WIFE. AFTER THAT HE QUIT SEX, SAYS JET HARRIS.

People

FOUR

Mrs Maria Travers was so incensed after her husband had bitten her on the buttocks that she tried to jump on him from a first floor window as he left the house.

Hartlepool Mail

FIVE

Mrs Woodbridge must have been the perfect wife for a huntsman. Before her marriage she had been a lady's maid, yet she readily adapted herself to kennel life.

Horse and Hound

UPPER CLASS SEX TECHNIQUE,
Most Typical Example of

It has long been a tradition of British life that the upper classes are allowed to discover the truth about the facts of life in their own way. Since this self-education usually involved a certain amount of clammy homosexual fumbling at public school and not much more, sexologists have always expected an astonishingly high percentage of serious erotic failure among these people.

After they marry, some of the brighter ex-public schoolboys notice that it's different with women — but this is not always the case. One peer was recently bemoaning the fact that his wife had failed to produce an heir after no less than three years of trying. A fellow member of his club took him aside and asked him one or two pertinent questions. Soon the problem was revealed.

'You've been using the tradesman's entrance, old boy,' said the friend carefully. 'Try the front door for a change.'

UTILITY PLAYER, *Busiest*

Speaking from a hiding-place in the German countryside, Mr Klaus Winter of the Mainz Meteors football club described a series of surprising off-the-ball incidents since he became president of the club.

'When I found my wife making love to Kipper Sazki, our striker, I forgave her for the team's sake,' said Dr Winter. 'Unfortunately, that was not the end of it. While I was out fund-raising or mixing cement for the new clubhouse, my wife slept with the whole team, then with the reserves, and then with the Old Boys Eleven. When the players heard that I was suing for divorce, they came round and tried to break my house to pieces.'

Dr Winter said that he was making use of his time in hiding to write his memoirs, *Football Fouls*.

With the aid of the traditional top hat and tennis racket handle, two Etonians attempt to master the facts of life

VENICE, *Oddest Claim to Fame of*

During the Middle Ages, Venice became famous among lovers for two things.

The first was the beauty and sexual availability of its nuns, who were praised and coveted throughout Europe. 'I really should stay with the nuns if I remained here,' wrote Charles de Brosses, Count of Tournai, in his journal. 'At this very moment, three of the city's convents are engaged in a passionate struggle to decide which of them is to have the honour of providing a mistress for the newly arrived Nuncio.'

De Brosses went on to describe a recent, much-publicized duel between two abbesses, who were both in love with the Abbé de Pomponne. They settled the matter in full religious garb, with stiletto swords.

More prosaically, Venice's other claim to fame was the widespread popularity of sodomy between lovers.

VENTURA, *Viviane*

>>> LOVE, *Most Broad-Minded Definition of.*

VERBOSE SEXUAL DESCRIPTION, *Most Confusing*

'At this explicit appeal Abu Shamat seized the girl by the thighs and aimed a great stick of conserve in the direction of the gate of triumphs; then, riding towards the crystal corridor, he halted at the gate of victories. After that he left the main road and spurred vigorously by a short cut to the mounter's door; but, as the nerve failed a little before the narrowness of this wicket, he turned then and, staving in the lid, found himself as much at home as if the architect had built on the actual measures of both. He continued his pleasant expedition, slowly visiting Monday market, the shops about Tuesday, Wednesday counter, and the stall of Thursday; then, when he had loosened all he had to loosen, he halted, like a good Mussulman, at the beginning of Friday.

'Such was the voyage of discovery which Abu Shamat and his little boy made in the garden of girlhood.'

The Tale of Ala al-Din Abu Shamat, 262nd night, *Arabian Nights.*

Verbose Sexual Description,
Second Most Confusing

'. . . and thereupon the Monk gave her a sound demonstration, as on double-bar feasts, with all the bob-majors customary in monasteries, psalms well sung in F major, candles ablaze, choirboys illuminating her on the Introit and also the Ite Missa Est, so that he withdrew at last, leaving her so sanctified that you could not have found a trace of the Wrath of the Lord in any part of that girl which had not been most amply monasticated.'

Balzac, *Droll Stories*, 'Concerning Brother Amader, glorious Abbot of Turpenay'.

A seventeenth century couple putting the rabbit out to feed

Verbose Sexual Description,
Third Most Confusing

'For three days they went at it without repose, showing the way the millrace flows, and how the industrious spindle goes. They gave the lamb suck, they startled the buck, they tried on the finger-ring for luck. They cradled the child, they kissed the twins, they polished the sword till it had not speck, they taught the sparrow how to peck, they made the camel show his neck, and fed the bird at the barley bins. They gave the little pigeon seed, and put the rabbit out to feed, with many another pretty deed, till they blew a hole in the shepherd's reed.'

Pastrycook's Tale, 848th Night, *Arabian Nights*.

VERSION OF THE BIBLE, *Shortest-lived*

There was only one error in the edition of the Bible produced by the printers Barker and Lucas during the reign of King James I, but it was enough to earn them a fine of £1000. Verse 14 in Exodus XX read 'Thou shalt commit adultery.'

Whether this was a misprint or a satirical comment on the moral standards of the day was never revealed.

VICTORIAN VALUES,
Most Frequently Forgotten

It's unlikely that, when Mrs Thatcher recently called for a return to the basic family values of the last century, she was thinking of the behaviour of the famous Victorian foreign secretary Lord Palmerston.

In an incident hushed up at the time, Palmerston was guilty of particularly vulgar breach of etiquette while staying with Queen Victoria at Windsor Castle — he tried to rape Mrs Susan Brand, one of Her Majesty's Ladies-in-Waiting. The Queen was said to be 'shocked by all measure' at this atrocious attempt.

Fortunately for Palmerston, Lord Melbourne (>>> **GOVERNMENT**, *Firmest Smack of*) intervened on his behalf and he was merely told to restrain himself in future.

VIRGIN BIRTH, *Least Divine*

When a fifteen-year-old barmaid from Lesotho in southern Africa was found to be pregnant, her doctor was somewhat surprised since the girl suffered from a rare congenital deformity which meant that she had no vagina.

'Curiosity could no longer be contained,' Dr Douwcouwe Verkuyl wrote in the *British Journal of Obstetrics and Gynaecology*, 'and she was interviewed with the help of a sympathetic nursing sister to ascertain how she could have conceived a child when normal sexual activity was obviously impossible.'

Eventually, the girl admitted that, nine months previously, she had been interrupted by a former lover while having oral sex with her new boyfriend. A fight ensued, during which she had been stabbed in the stomach. While the wound was being operated on, sperm had leaked from the stomach and had been washed up the fallopian tube — with miraculous consequences.

WAR HERO, *Prissiest*

One of the safest hiding places for fugitive Allied airmen shot down in France during the Second World War was the local brothel. Not only did it frequently possess a network of secret passages and escape routes but it was also rarely raided by the local police who believed that to interrupt a man while he was making love risked him suffering permanent psychological damage.

For this reason, many English airmen evaded arrest by acting as clients whenever the brothels received a visit from the local police.

But not all of them. One young airman was so horrified by the idea of consorting with a prostitute, even to save his life, that he refused. When news reached the brothel where he was hiding that a raid was imminent, he was dressed up as one of the girls.

Unfortunately, a trace of stubble on his chin gave him away and he was arrested on the spot.

WEDDING ADVICE, *Least Positive*

The moral philosopher and writer Sydney Smith was said to be one of the greatest conversationalists of the early nineteenth century, but sometimes his wit verged on the cruel.

On hearing that a young Scottish friend of his was to marry a woman of sizeable proportions, he cried, 'Going to marry her? Impossible! You mean a part of her; he could not marry all himself. It would be a case, not of bigamy, but trigamy; the neighbourhood or magistrates should interfere. There is enough of her to furnish wives for the whole parish. One man marry her! It is monstrous! You might people a colony with her; or give an assembly with her; or perhaps take your morning walk around her, always provided there are frequent resting places, and you were in rude health. I once was rash enough to try walking round her before breakfast, but only got half-way and gave it up exhausted. Or you might read the Riot Act and disperse her; in short, you might do anything but marry her!'

WEDDING DAYS, *Five Worst*

ONE

Asked by a court in Nashville, Tennessee why he was suing his wife for divorce after only a month of married life, Willard Roberts claimed that he had been the worse for wear on their wedding day, having consumed two gallons of beer.

Despite his inebriated state, he managed to explain to his bride Lisa that he had decided not to go through with the ceremony. It was then that she knocked him down and sat on him until he agreed to marry her.

Lisa, who weighs sixteen and a half stone, told the court, 'I still love him.'

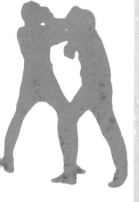

TWO

At the height of celebrations at a wedding reception in China, the groom kissed his new bride passionately on the neck. After a few moments, the girl collapsed and died. At the inquest, doctors revealed that the duration, passion and generally over-enthusiastic nature of the kiss had caused heart palpitations — with tragic results.

THREE

It was when his wedding reception was in full swing that Martin Chapman made a particularly shocking public announcement. After climbing on a chair and calling for silence, he said, 'I am sorry everyone. I cannot live with a woman. I am gay.' He then opened his shirt to show love-bites that he had been given by his boyfriend. In the ensuing chaos, his bride, Karon, grabbed him by the lapels of his wedding suit and blacked both his eyes.

Commenting later, Karon said, 'I shall be very busy in the next few days. I have got to be tested for AIDS, start annulment proceedings, and look into the prospects for an abortion.'

FOUR

A big wedding can be something of a mixed blessing for brides on the island of Marquesas in the Caribbean.

It is the local tradition that, after the ceremony, the bride should lie down with her head on her new husband's lap. The guests at the ceremony then form an orderly queue — elders and social inferiors at the front, tribal chiefs at the back — and take it in turns to introduce her to the joys of married life. When all the guests have drifted away, satisfied, the husband may consummate the marriage.

The esteem in which a wife is held in Marquesas depends on one key question: how long was the queue at her wedding?

FIVE

At the other end of the scale, the honeymoon night of crooning family entertainer Des O'Connor was rather less interesting. His wife Gillian later told friends that she had spent it 'chatting to friends and sipping cocoa.' Des explained that he had always wanted his marriage 'to be like a scene from *The Sound of Music.*'

WELSH TOWN, *Most Rapidly Expanding*

A GP consulted by a male patient with a boil on his groin was mildly surprised to note that he had the letters LDO tatooed on his penis. Having analysed the problem, the doctor sent the man to have the boil lanced by a nurse.

'Good Lord, doctor,' the nurse commented later. 'Did you see where that man had Llandudno tattooed?'

WEST, *Mae*

>>> STATISTICAL APPENDIX.

WILSON, *Edmund*

| >>> CRITIC, *Most Confused.*

WITNESS, *Most Surprising*

Persistent sexual misbehaviour finally caught up with Malden carpenter William Buckman, according to the Massachusetts court reports of 1674. He was arraigned in court for 'shamefull lasciviousness in his words and actions towards fourteen married women.'

Witnesses told the court that Buckman cast his net wide and had propositioned newlyweds, grandmothers, maids and, on two occasions, church sisters. He had told Goodwife Elizabeth Webb that 'she was a pretty roague and made his hart leap in his britches', had offered Rebecca West two bushels of wheat (belonging to someone else) 'to have his will of her' and had snatched kisses, felt legs and 'grabbed on to laps' of women throughout the parish.

There was only one witness for the defence — Buckman's wife. Claiming that one of her husband's alleged victims, Elizabeth Payne, was behind the plot, she revealed that on one occasion Payne 'had pulled the chair from under him as he sat by the fire and puld meat out of his hand as he sat at meat and beat the pott to his head as he had been drinking.'

Buckman was found guilty and fined £25.

# WOOLF, *Virginia*
>>> **MATING RITUALS**, *Ten Least Romantic.*

WORK,
Sexologist Most Frequently Interrupted while at

In his scholarly work *Oriental Orgies*, J. Cleugh uncharacteristically allows personal research experience to colour his judgement of the modern Egyptian.

'From a European or North American point of view,' he writes, 'the girls and boys darken their already sun-browned cheeks too much, chatter excessively during copulation and are prone to interrupt it, for reasons incomprehensible to anyone but an Egyptian, too often.'

Mr Cleugh does not explain how he reached this conclusion.

# WRIGHT, *Fiona*
>>> **STATISTICAL APPENDIX**.

X-RATED PURPLE PASSAGES, *Five Least Erotic*

ONE

On the northern coast of Cornwall, very quiet although we were only five hundred yards from the sea, in our bedroom, I knelt and watched my penis pucker the thin scarlet lips of her vagina. They received me rather like the flaps of a security-screening machine at an airport. N., biting the side of one hand, watched on the screen of her closed eyelids the passage of the contents.

I knelt and serviced her apparatus with the most delicate attention; until she was peeled back from herself into emptiness, her limbs bewildered, her eyes full of the strange panic of stampede. 'How well you know me!' A high priestess, with a vision of cataclysm, farting and crying, beside herself with the glorious humiliation of pleasure.

I felt that I was becoming increasingly unreal.

Richard Thornley, *The Dark Clarinet*, (1988)

TWO

At the Radcliffe Camera I summoned up my courage to go and ask the tall, mammoth-breasted desk clerk if she would like to come to tea. To my astonishment she said yes. I sported my oak, for the first time. As I worked my fingers inside her wet vagina, she seemed like a beached whale. She hinted that it could be safe — I could withdraw. But something held me back: maybe love or loyalty. 'Well, I suppose it's not very satisfactory,' she murmured. 'I must have a pee,' she said after we had finished our heavy petting. 'It has that effect, doesn't it?' I didn't know; I knew almost nothing about sex. She used the chamber-pot in my bedroom. I saw her once more, taking her to the pictures; but she seemed altogether too big, and I let the tide wash her off.

I sported my oak again when Maureen came up for a summer visit. . . .

D.M. Thomas, *Memories and Hallucinations*, (1988)

FOUR

I began to wonder if even my trusty henchman could take much more of this. Vinnie's cunt was as special as the rest of her. Where Heather's was big and generous and welcoming, Vinnie's was narrow and voracious. Not only was it as long and close-fitting as a glove-finger, it was totally prehensile, varying the pressure of its silken clutch from second to second and from inch to inch of its unusual length. I had known already that Vinnie was in the habit of thinking with her cunt, but now I realized that she could also talk with it, and what she wordlessly told me went into the marrow of my bones and corpuscles of my blood and the cells of my flesh and drove me insane for ever.

John Wain, *Where The Rivers Meet*

THREE

His bollocks were the size of duck eggs, and you could have used his scrotum for a bathing cap.

Sergeant W. Kent in a letter to *Fiesta*

FIVE

I lay beside her. She was like a warm lozenge. Her hands went to my thing.

Leslie Thomas

YETI, *Silliest*

Reported sightings in China of a small, hairy creature, looking like the legendary yeti, have recently been confirmed. A 3′8″ wild man was captured by villagers in a remote mountain region. According to press reports, he was 'attempting to tease a woman' at the time.

YUPPY LOVE, *Least Typical Instance of*

Psychologists have frequently expressed concern that the modern young executive has become so obsessed with the quest for money, status and at least two powerphones in the Porsche, that sex has lost all appeal for them.

Such is not the problem for the young Saudi Arabian millionaire Saleh-el-Modiia. With four wives to keep happy, Saleh decided to feed the details of his love-life into a computer and leave it to sort out his schedule.

As a result, he visits his first wife on Monday, having first checked her details on the computer — birthday, favourite colour, individual quirks — then travels about the country to see his other three wives. On Friday, he spends the day working on his computer business, Saturday he devotes to the children and on Sunday he takes a well-earned rest.

Unfortunately, Saleh has been unable to keep pace with his high-tech schedule. 'The computer has gone haywire,' one of his wives wrote in a Riyadh newspaper. 'It's making Saleh too exhausted — he just falls asleep in my arms.'

Replying to these allegations, Saleh said he would never get rid of the computer. 'It's only gone wrong once,' he said. That was when I was in hospital and all four wives came to visit me at the same time.'

ZEALOT, *Dottiest*

Speaking to local journalists, Councillor Gwilym Rowlands of Caenarvonshire has explained his call for revising the school curriculum to include more religious teaching. While admitting that religious education was being given in schools, he asked whether it went far enough. The Ten Commandments, he said, contained the basis of sex education.

ZIPPED-UP FIRST NIGHT,
Most Definitively

It was an uneventful overnight trip on the ferry from the Hook of Holland for Chief Officer Mike Rice until he received an emergency call to one of the first-class cabins. Somewhat surprised, since he knew that the cabin was occupied by a couple who had just got married, Rice hurried along to find out what the problem was.

'There he was met by a scene that shook him,' skipper Bill Bramhill was later to tell a press conference. 'The groom was standing with his treasured assets well and truly caught in the zip fastener and his bride was wringing her hands in dismay.'

It was here that Bramhill's naval training stood him in good stead. Judging that the situation required expert medical attention, he cut around the zip, leaving it attached to the bridegroom, and wrapped the above-mentioned treasured assets in a bandage. As soon as the ferry docked the next morning, the man was rushed to hospital, where he was freed under a local anaesthetic.

The couple told awaiting reporters that they wished to remain anonymous.

ZODIAC, *Least Publicized Origin of the Twelve Signs of the*

It is believed among certain religious groups in India that the Lingam of the god Siva was so mighty that it was cut into twelve parts in order to give birth to all living creatures. The signs of the zodiac also originated from this supernatural event.

STATISTICAL APPENDIX: *Pathetic Boasters who Honestly Believe that Quantity is More Important than Quality*

Those impressed by the ridiculous, fumbling romance between Fiona Wright, Queen of the Bimbos, and ageing millionaire Sir Ralph Halpern, simply because it was claimed they made love five times in one night, should remember the First Rule of Sexology: *Quantity, like size, is entirely irrelevant.*

In fact, research has shown that the more someone brags about their performance in bed, the worse they are likely to be.

Bearing this in mind, here is a list of some of the lousiest lovers in human history.

Number of times achieved (allegedly) in a twelve hour period

80

In the great work of Arabian history, *The Fabulous Feats of the Futtering Freebooters*, it is claimed that Abu'l-Hayjeh once deflowered eighty virgins in one night. Since the same work claimed that Abu'l Hayluck could remain erect for thirty days and, even less pleasantly, Felah the Negro 'did jerk off his yard for all of a week', sexologists remain sceptical as to its precise accuracy.

30

Empress Theodora, the wife of the sixth century Roman Emperor Justinian I, appointed herself 'the protectress of faithless wives' and enjoyed picnicking outside the gates of Rome where, according to contemporary reports, she would 'open the gates of Venus to ten men'. The next day, she would take on their thirty servants. Because of the strict twelve hour ruling, only the servants can be included in this analysis.

20

When two of history's great sexual braggarts and fantasists, Frank Harris and Guy de Maupassant, met, they vied with one another as to which of them was the most irresistible. De Maupassant ran out an easy winner, having claimed that he had made love to six women one after another in a brothel, a feat that was observed by fellow novelist Gustave Flaubert. When Harris asked how many times he could make love in one night, the Frenchman shrugged modestly and said, 'I've counted twenty or more.'

13

King David was reported to have achieved this on at least one occasion.

12

When asked who her best lover was, Mae West claimed that she had once spent a day in bed with a man who made love twenty-four times — and she had counted the used condoms to prove it.

Casanova's record was twelve times (with the same woman) on one day.

Casanova: Next!

In the eighteenth century, the Prince de Condé, Louis Francois de Bourbon, was so delighted at having had his mistress Mme Deschamps twelve times in one night that he had all his buttons and shirts imprinted and marked with the number twelve, bought twelve guns and twelve swords, ordered twelve table settings to be laid for every meal, took 1200 francs pocket money every week and, when he went out, tipped twelve beggars on the street.

10

King Chou-hsin of the Shang Dynasty (1558–1302BC) was said to have 'ten healthy and strong women in a row every night.' Eight foot tall, he also enjoyed killing tigers with his bare hands and showed off to his visitors by walking around the room, carrying a lover on the mighty royal member.

Discovered by Captain Cook, King Lapetamaka of the Tonga Islands regarded it as his regal duty to deflower every virgin on the islands. Even when in his eighties, he found time to do this eight to ten times every day.

9

Later to become a relentless philanderer (when he died, the brothels of Paris went into official mourning), Victor Hugo was a virgin until the age of twenty. Then, on his marriage night, he managed it nine times.

Victor: an unlikely philanderer

8

The greatest of all nineteenth century '*grande horizontales*', La Bella Otero, slept her way round most of the royal families of Europe, acquiring vast wealth, but her greatest love was Aristide Briand, who could give her nothing but love — sometimes up to eight times a night.

6

In his youth, Charlie Chaplin used to boast that he could achieve six 'bouts' in quick succession. All he needed, he said, was a five-minute break between each one.

According to her ex-boyfriend, sexy Sam Fox has done it six times a night. This account is regarded as particularly unreliable since it was the ex-boyfriend who did it with her.

5

Sir Ralph Halpern with Fiona Wright (>>> **NASAL SEX**, *Most Publicized Case of*).

King Louis of Bavaria was so pleased when Lola Montez 'caused him to achieve ten orgasms in a twenty-four hour period' that he gave her his kingdom.

The Kinsey report includes a man who had made love thirty-three times a week over a period of thirty years. The eminent sexologist calculated that this amounted to a total of 52,000 times or five times a day.

James Boswell proudly reported that, during a night spent with Louise, one of his mistresses, he 'was fairly lost in rapture no less than five times and the worthy Louise called me a prodigy.' Boswell's other vital statistics included: illegitimate children — five; cases of the clap — nineteen.

4

Joan Collins told friends that the reason she had broken off her affair with Warren Beatty was that she had become tired of his incessant sexual demands. Four times a day was his average.

3

Although King Ibn Saud had a mere three women a night, he is worth including in the analysis because he kept up this schedule without fail (except during battles) between the age of eleven and his death in 1953 at the age of seventy-two.

9 times in ten years

Leading social observer Serena Gray has insisted that this statistic represents some sort of record.

Number of lovers (allegedly) seduced

16,257

The eighteenth-century actress and good-time girl Mlle Dubois made a catalogue of her lovers over the years. Her score rate averaged at over three a day.

10,000

Yet another French boaster, Georges Simenon, claimed to have seduced this number of women during his life.

5,000

Ninon de Lenclos (1620–1705) was said to have slept with this number of men — interestingly, one tenth of them belonged to the clergy. She embarked on her last affair, with the Abbé de Geduyn, at the age of eighty.

3,000 (in a year)

Winston Mboto Dhuluo has recently been appointed official lover to the Kikuyu tribe in Kenya, a job which entails defloreating at least one thousand virgins a year and satisfying any Kikuyu woman, however old or unattractive, who is feeling sexually restless. It is estimated that, at peak periods, Dhuluo is obliged to work on eighty women a week and up to three thousand in a year. His initiation ceremony — a public thrashing outside the lair of a hyena — was filmed for Australian television.

Sarah: a good effort

1,000

Sarah Bernhardt claimed that her score was well into four figures.

760

More impressive than it might appear, this achievement by King Solomon included seven hundred wives and sixty mistresses.

Conclusions of in-depth statistical analysis

1. The French are the biggest liars in the world.
2. Those who keep the score are almost certainly not concentrating on the job in hand.
3. Members of the British royal family have some catching up to do to compare with their counterparts abroad.

BIBLIOGRAPHY

While researching this book, I made repeated pillaging raids on *Punch*'s 'Country Life' column and Christopher Logue's 'True Stories' in *Private Eye*. I also used Fritz Spiegl's article on doubles-entendres and misunderstandings, published in the *Listener* of 8th August, 1985.

John Atkins, *Sex in Literature* (John Calder, 1978)

L. Basserman, *The Oldest Profession* (Arthur Barker, 1967)

Simon Bell, Richard Curtis and Helen Fielding, *Who's Had Who* (Faber & Faber, 1987)

Paul F. Boller Jr and Ronald L. Davis, *Hollywood Anecdotes* (Macmillan, 1988)

P.G. Bouce (ed.), *Sexuality in Eighteenth-Century Britain*, (Manchester University Press, 1982)

Gerald C. Clarke, *Capote; a Biography* (Hamish Hamilton, 1988)

J. Cleugh, *Love Locked Out* (Blond, 1963)

J. Cleugh, *Oriental Orgies* (Blond & Briggs, 1968)

Cleugh, Taylor, Dwyer and Dwyer, *How D'You Do?* (Pallas, 1939)

Dr Robert Clifford, *Not There, Doctor* (Pelham, 1978)

Jilly Cooper, *Class* (Methuen, 1979)

Jilly Cooper (ed.), *The British in Love* (Arlington, 1980)

John Costello, *Love, Sex and War* (Collins, 1985)

L. Cunliffe, C. Brown and J. Connell, *The Dirty Bits* (André Deutsch, 1981)

H. Cutner, *A Short History of Sex-Worship* (Watts & Co, 1940)

Som Deva, *The Marching Eros* (Anuj Publications, 1983)

Kirk Douglas, *The Ragman's Son* (Simon & Schuster, 1988)

Anna Ford, *Men* (Weidenfeld & Nicolson, 1985)

Peter Gardella, *Innocent Ecstasy* (OUP, 1985)

Robert Goldenson and Kenneth Anderson, *Everything You Ever Wanted To Know About Sex But Never Dared Ask* (Bloomsbury, 1986)

Jonathon Green, *Days in the Life* (Heinemann, 1988)

Richard Huggett, *Bedside Sex* (Fontana, 1985)

Steve Humphries, *A Secret World of Sex* (Sidgwick & Jackson, 1988)

Paul Johnson, *Intellectuals* (Weidenfeld & Nicolson, 1988)

Patrick J. Kearney, *The Private List* (Jay Landesman, 1981)

Michael Korda, *Charmed Lives* (Allen Lane, 1980)

Chris Lloyd (ed.), *The Fiesta Letters* (Star, 1986)

Brigid McConville and John Shearlaw, *The Slanguage of Sex*, (Macdonald, 1984)

H. Montgomery Hyde, *A Tangled Web* (Constable, 1980)

Malcolm Muggeridge, *Tread Softly for you Tread on my Jokes* (Collins, 1966)

John Osborne, *A Better Class of Person* (Methuen, 1981)

Lawrence Paros, *The Erotic Tongue* (Arlington, 1988)

Guy Philipps, *Bad Behaviour* (Elm Tree, 1988)

Fiona Pitt-Kethley, *Journeys to the Underworld* (Chatto and Windus, 1988)

Gordon Rattray Taylor, *Sex in History* (Thames & Hudson, 1963)

Nigel Rees, *A Year of Boobs and Blunders* (Unwin Paperbacks, 1984)

Shelley Ross, *Washington Babylon* (Allison & Busby, 1988)

Alan Rusbridger, *A Concise History of the Sex Manual 1886-1986* (Faber & Faber, 1986)

Patricia Seaton Lawford, *Peter Lawford* (Sidgwick & Jackson, 1988)

Dyan Sheldon and Judy Allen, *Picking on Men Again* (Arrow, 1986)

G.L. Simons, *The Book of World Sexual Records* (Virgin, 1982)

D.M. Thomas, *Memories and Hallucinations* (Gollancz, 1988)

R. Thompson, *Sex in Middlesex* (University of Massachusetts Press, 1986)

Irving Wallace, David Wallechinsky, Amy Wallace and Sylvia Wallace, *The Intimate Sex Lives of Famous People* (Hutchinson, 1981)

David Wallechinsky, Irving Wallace and Amy Wallace, *The Book of Lists* (Cassell, 1977)

CREDITS